VOLUME

VOL UME

Patrick Kooiman

LANNOO

Contents

Love a Little Rummage

Finding Vintage Furniture

Vintage collector and shop owner Babette Kulik

Madonna once offered her a job as her personal shopper – but Babette Kulik politely turned down the Queen of Pop. Instead, she would much rather stay in London to buy and sell her own vintage furniture and books, thank you very much. If you're in the area, be sure to drop by and ask Babette all about her particular nose for the rarest finds.

Clash of Ages

Smart Art Buying

Gallerist Flore de Brantes

Where do you start if you want to buy good art? And no, I'm not thinking of a framed poster at the mall. I'm talking Art with a capital 'A' here, Art that moves you – that once-in-a-lifetime piece that makes your room. To find out the answer, let's meet up with one of the most original and authentic gallerists you'll ever meet: Flore de Brantes.

Expert Advice from Interior Decorator Thong Lei

Bouquets, Nature and Decay

Picking Flowers

Florist Michael Swier

Outspoken. Enigmatic. Flamboyant. Those are the three first things that come to mind when I think of Michael Swier. Not necessarily words you would associate with a florist, but then again Michael doesn't own your average flower shop. Together with his former partner René, he runs Zomers, the *non plus ultra* when it comes to luscious flowers, avant-garde vases and jaw-dropping home accessories. What's his secret? And how do you make sure flowers add maximum oomph to any interior? Let's find out!

Slowly Moving Rocks

Feeling Zen with Trends

Journalist and trend watcher Candida Zanelli

No wonder she is a fixture in *AD China*! I meet up with Candida Zanelli, who is one of the best interior stylists in the world. Candida takes me on a tour of the annual Salone del Mobile in Milan and tells me how interior-design trends are born and how you can incorporate them in your own home. After all, Milan is still the epicenter of cool when it comes to kick-ass interior design.

The Only Trend Is…That There Is No Trend
Judith van Mourik Agrees with Candida Zanelli

Sugar, Spice and All Things Nice

The Art of Hosting

Food historian Tasha Marks

So, now that you've read how to build your own colorful and sophisticated interior, all that remains is one final question: what good is it if you don't have any friends to share it with? Invite them over, throw a party and serve delicious food and drinks with showmanship. Yes, you can be the host – or hostess – with the mostest! But where do you start? Let's go to London to find out the answer from food historian Tasha Marks.

Volume

What if your interior could speak, tell its own story? What would that story be? I bet you would want it to be rich, exciting, with unexpected twists and turns. Now look around your living room. If you're not happy with what you see, well, congratulations! You have so bought the right book, it's not even funny anymore.

As an interior-design blogger with more than a few makeovers under my belt, I wanted to find out how to do them properly. Because let me tell you, I've made a few mistakes along the way. And I want you to avoid them.

And so, I set out on trip around Western Europe to meet up with nine interior-design and art professionals who I truly admire. Not only did they share their best tips and tricks, but they also told their life story. And it all became clear to me: your interior should be a reflection of your own life story!

One of the people I learned about along the way was Queen Maria Pia of Portugal. Although she died a long time ago, she made me realize that we all want to create an interior that just works – no matter what age we live in. You see, as Maria Pia got older, she had a vision. Of a monastery that she would turn into the ultimate mansion, called Bussaco Palace. That dream never came true. The monastery became a hotel instead. And I stayed there along the way, contemplating what it is that I want to tell you in this book. What all nine people I interviewed for this book have in common is that they don't follow trends. They dance to the beat of their own drum – and so should you.

I like to think that I have some of that spirit myself. After all, who in their right mind paints their entire living room bright pink? At night, I like to sit in my favorite chair, look around me and think to myself: 'Yup, this is totally me!' And I really, really want you to develop that feeling as well.

Good interiors don't have to cost an arm and a leg. Sure, it can help if you're awash in cash – but in the end, it doesn't matter. Your home should be colorful and sophisticated. And I firmly believe you can do that on any budget if you just read the interviews carefully and apply what you've read.

There is one last thing that I feel I need to share with you. And that is that you should stop looking online for interior-design inspiration. At the top of your Pinterest feed, you are most likely to see the most middle-of-the-road interiors. Neither should you watch TV shows about interior design. They are bland, tend to go for the lowest common denominator and are often sponsored.

For now, let me thank you from the bottom of my heart for buying this book. I have written and photographed it with all my heart, and I hope it shows. Time to turn up the volume!

Patrick

We're All Stories

Storytelling at Home
Studio MHNA

Every good interior starts with a story. A concept, if you will. But where do you begin? And how do you develop the story you want to tell? If your head is spinning after two questions already, then by all means sit down, relax and take a load off. Because I have found the two very best master storytellers, self-proclaimed *scénaristes d'intérieur,* to get you started. Can I introduce you to Marc Hertrich and Nicolas Adnet from Studio MHNA in Paris? These two men design luxury hotel interiors all over the world. And although that may sound very fancy-schmancy, constantly developing new concepts for the ever-changing world of hospitality can be a daunting task. The biggest challenge Marc and Nicolas faced, however, came when they were asked to come up with a design for Madame Jeanne Augier, the eccentric woman who has most inspired them. Her hotel, the iconic Negresco on Boulevard des Anglais in Nice, is the ultimate expression of a life story told through interior design. And although your own interior makeover probably won't be on the scale of the Negresco, I still bet you have something meaningful to say. In the end, we're all stories.

We like it when an unusual combination of items tells a great story.

Marc started his rhino collection when he backpacked through Thailand once. 'The idea for me is not to buy as many rhinos as possible. You should only add new items to your collection if they're made from a material you don't have yet. I have a rare crystal rhino from Baccarat, but also one I bought on the beach in Ubud.'

Life at Lanvin

Nicolas, before you tell me everything about telling stories through interior design, what's your own life story?

My story starts in a small town east of Paris, with my mother working at the local hospital and my father earning a living as a car salesman. An average family, as you can tell. My sister was my true role model. She was ten years older, very ambitious and decided to move to Paris as soon as she could to work in the fashion industry. When I was 13 years old, she thought it would be a good idea to take me to my first fashion show. It was a show by Dietmar Sterling and I remember it to this day. The lights went out, the music started playing and for the next hour a world of perfect beauty unfolded right in front of me. It was unreal. Until now, I cannot find the words to describe the experience. I did, however, realize that this was where I belonged and so I enrolled in fashion school. The first year turned out to be way too technical for my taste, unfortunately. And to be honest, I was much more interested in enjoying everything the nightlife in Paris had to offer. I dropped out of school after a huge argument with my father. He laid down one condition: I didn't have to move back home if I managed to find a job. Which was fine by me, because I figured out at an early age that when you want something in life, studying for it is only one of the paths you can travel. Through a friend, I found a job at the Lanvin store: three hours a day to replace the manager during lunch, plus Saturdays and Mondays. After I started, I quickly realized this wasn't exactly a busy supermarket job. And so I started helping out the art director of the women's fashion show. If that wasn't enough, I would hang out in my spare time at the ateliers of other haute-couture houses to learn as much as I could. That is how I went behind the scenes of the fashion world.

I never knew you could do that! How did you get in?

Things were a bit less secretive with *sur mesure* for men. I would have lunch with someone who worked there and then invite myself over for a look. I learned all about fabrics that way. With women's wear, it was a totally different story. Not even the chairman of Lanvin could see the collection before it hit the runway. Soon after I started working there as the assistant to the CEO, I also struck up a friendship with Mademoiselle Michelle, who at the time was the 60-something head seamstress at Lanvin with her very own secret atelier. I used to spend hours there, learning how she would convert a simple sketch by Claude Montana into this perfectly curved dress out of nothing more than mousseline – an impossible fabric to work with. Montana would have these fantastic but totally unrealistic ideas. 'I want a dress that looks like a cloudy Parisian sky,' he'd say and then Mademoiselle Michelle would work her magic and pull it off using six or seven different fabrics to create just the right amount of volume. She taught me that nothing is ever impossible. There is always a solution to a problem; all you have to do is find it by working very, very hard. It was also the first time I learned how you can come up with a story and translate it into an actual design.

Work Hard, Play Hard

And you, Marc, what's your story?

I grew up in the Alsace in a family that had been making cabinets for six generations. My parents, aunts, uncles and cousins were all very much interested in the arts and in furniture design in particular. The family member who influenced me the most, however, was my grandfather – even though he died before I was born. He was a true *homo universalis*. In his free time he traveled all over Europe, he was a great cook, a talented painter and quite an interesting photographer. All the stories I heard about him inspired me to start drawing myself. At school, I learned how to become a cabinetmaker myself. At night, I would take drawing lessons at the École Supérieure des Arts Décoratifs in Strasbourg. Some of the professors liked my work and suggested I continue my studies at École Boulle, the famous design school in Paris. Everyone there was so passionate. We worked hard, but we also played hard …

Can you imagine what this bedroom would have looked like if the ceiling had been left white? You can bet it wouldn't look half as sophisticated as it does now.

What were the most valuable lessons you learned at École Boulle?

You have to study the history of art and then take the most important elements of the past and make them modern in a creative way. My breakthrough project was at La Malmaison, a Napoleonic chateau that I decorated with twentieth-century pieces by Eileen Gray and Andrée Putman – two designers I still admire. I also have some very warm memories of Jean-Maurice Simoneau, who taught color theory at École Boulle for over 33 years. He taught me you can tell amazing stories in your interior with colors. Our current loft apartment, for instance, has a big living room with three adjoining rooms on the side that look like boxes. We gave each room its own distinct color so that they each tell their own story. I love sitting in our turquoise kitchen and looking through our deep purple bedroom at our Yves Klein blue workroom at the other end.

So what did you do after you graduated?

After I graduated, I did some interior design work for Michel Boyer. And it was through him that I caught my big break designing for Le Richemond in Geneva, which was still an independent and family-owned hotel at the time. My assignment was supposed to last three months only but I ended up staying four years. Every day, I had lunch with either the concierge, the *gouvernante*, the butler or the housekeepers. They taught me everything you have to look after to run a world-famous hotel on a daily basis. After all, things could get quite hectic behind the scenes with guests like Michael Jackson and the King of Saudi Arabia. Money certainly wasn't a dirty word in the 1980s and I loved the opulence of it all. Le Richemond also had a very friendly atmosphere. I remember how the concierge used to joke with all the celebrities. That was a true lesson to me. To this day, our work is luxurious yet playful. We mix sophisticated pieces with very simple things. I like it when an unusual combination of items tells a great story. You shouldn't be afraid to improvise at home. Add some fantasy, you'll know intuitively if it works or not.

Marc and Nicholas live in a loft apartment with three adjoining rooms on the side that look like boxes. They gave each room its own distinct color so that they each tell their own story: turquoise, deep purple and Yves Klein blue.

Like in the movies

Nicolas, how did you two meet?

We met thanks to a mutual friend. For about five years he kept going on about how we had to meet because he was sure we would hit it off. And then one day, he called me and said: 'I'm sitting on a café terrace with Marc and you have to come now!' And so I did. It was like in the movies. Love at first sight. We've been together for over 20 years now.

Why did your mutual friend think you'd fit so well together?

For starters, we both had purple walls in our apartments. At the time, everyone loved that minimalist *wenge* Christian Liaigre style, and so purple and emerald were not the most obvious colors to use. We also shared a passion for exotic pieces and combining them in original ways.

So tell me, Nicolas, how did go from having a relationship to working together?

To be honest, I started helping out simply by cooking for everyone. I moved in with Marc pretty quickly. And when I would come home from work at Lanvin, Marc would often still be working on a project with his team. You see, his studio was also our apartment. And then one night, Marc and his team started working on the design for a new restaurant called La Gare that was going to be located in an old railway station. Marc asked me to make a selection of colors and materials and I jumped at the opportunity. The owner had already bought six huge surrealist paintings. I studied them very closely and then created a mood board with colors and materials I thought would match the paintings and the location. It became the starting point for the design of La Gare. Creating a mood board is a great way to visualize your research.

I love the parallel of how you started your career in fashion by working the cash register and then embarked upon a professional interior-design career by … cooking?

Yes, I started two professional careers without a formal education! I started at square one with Marc. I thought I'd give it six months to see if it worked and here we are! People come to Studio MHNA because we are interior scenarists. Telling stories is probably what I'm best at. And I can tell you that works very well for anyone who wants to change their interior. Tell your own story!

The Negresco tells the story of *la douce France* through interior design. And that story, of course, would not be complete without Napoleon Bonaparte.

The Story of Maria Felix

Okay, then! But how do you go about telling your own story?

We have the opportunity to work in many different countries and so the first thing we do when we start on a project is to research the history of the place we're going to be working on. That research is the basis of the stories we tell in our work. It can be very literal, but sometimes it also works to just convey an emotion. But no matter the story, we like to add craziness. So much so, in fact, that presenting a design to a client can be a nerve-racking experience. I remember vividly when I had to tell Henri Giscard d'Estaing, the director of Club Med, that we wanted to design its new resort in Mexico around this famous Mexican 1950s movie actress called Maria Felix. We developed our idea by imagining her living in a big house by

the sea and inviting people to stay over. We had dedicated each restaurant at the resort to one aspect of her life. For instance, we wanted a glamorous restaurant filled with crystal chandeliers and white mousseline draperies. But then we would set it off with another restaurant at the very end of the resort garden that Maria Felix would use to serve Mexican specialties for her closest friends. When our presentation was over, we were met with total silence. Everybody looked at Henri and after a while, he said: *'J'adore le glamour!'* I can tell you, that was quite a relief.

What do you like about designing hospitality?

Hotel and restaurant owners always expect new ideas. They want to keep surprising their guests and that is why they appreciate the creativity that goes into our designs. Hotels in particular have become destinations in themselves – they are no longer just a place to spend the night. Striving for that element of surprise doesn't mean we follow trends, however. And it's definitely not something you want to do if you want to design your own interior in a meaningful way. I remember this interior design journalist who had visited our apartment in Paris. She loved the place but when we ran into her a year later she thought it had gone out of style. 'Too many colors', was her verdict. But we didn't care. We are what we are. And if that meant we would stay a small agency, then so be it. We have never been into a Zen minimalist style and so we avoid projects that require that particular style. We would only make a bad copy. I guess knowing what you're good at also means understanding what you're maybe not so good at.

Hotel owners always expect new ideas. That is why Marc and Nicolas think hotels are a great source of inspiration for your own home. Le Negresco's Bar combines a tapestry from 1683 with fresh flowers hanging from the ceiling. Wouldn't you love to do something similar at home?

The One and Only Jeanne Augier

Let's stick to what you're really good at, like the rooms you designed for the legendary Hotel Negresco in Nice. That must have been quite a project, Nicolas!

Yes, it was quite the challenge. You see, the Negresco is one of the last remaining independent five-star hotels in the world. It is owned by Jeanne Augier, an interior design legend who still lives on the sixth floor of the hotel. Madame Augier is in her 90s now and designing the Negresco has been her life's work. It is filled to the brim with an amazing collection of furniture, art and antiques from all the different eras of French history. Salvador Dalí was one of Madame Augier's best friends. You can see some of his works at the hotel. Jean-Pierre Yvaral custom-designed the pattern on the carpets in the hallways of the hotel.

What makes the Negresco so special for you, Marc?

To me, getting the opportunity to design for a mythical hotel like the Negresco was Studio MHNA's crowning achievement. It was a boutique hotel before the word was even invented. I also feel very emotionally attached to the Negresco. Unlike Le Richemond in Geneva, the Negresco today is still independent and that gives it a professional yet charming atmosphere you won't find anywhere else in the world. It is something we strive for in our own work. Like Madame Augier, we don't follow trends. Instead, we let our imagination run wild and mix up furniture and art from many different eras.

Versailles: the word alone conjures up visions of insane opulence and luxury. Don't decorate your entire home like *le Roi Soleil.* That would be overkill! But what's keeping you from buying a nice Louis XIV chair, painting it gold and then having it reupholstered in sumptuous silk?

Some people think Madame Augier doesn't even care what they think about her style.

And what about you, Nicolas?

The Negresco is one of the most overwhelming personal expressions in interior design in the world. The contradictions in the interior design of the Negresco are stunning, there are so many different styles and colors all mixed together. You can imagine that designing rooms for a hotel like that requires a delicate approach. We immersed ourselves in Madame Augier's world, analyzed her work and then came to the only logical conclusion – and that is that we had to respect Madame first and foremost, to pay tribute to her by showing guests a vision of what a new creation from her hand would look like. The last thing we wanted to do was to make a reproduction.

This giant Baccarat chandelier in the Royal Lounge was originally ordered by Emperor Nicholas II right before the Russian Revolution. Needless to say, he never picked it up.

How did you make sure your work would not end up like a reproduction?

The biggest pitfall to avoid was simply doing a Dalí room, an Yvaral room and then say, Look, a tribute to Madame Augier. That would have been too easy. When you analyze the Negresco closely, it is the mix of seemingly unmixable styles and items that makes it unique. Some people think Madame Augier doesn't even care what they think about her style. The Negresco is her place, plain and simple. We took elements from the hotel, like the Louis XVI chairs in the Versailles room and then redesigned them for our time. And because Madame Augier had a special relationship with so many artists when she was younger, we asked a very respectable Parisian art gallery to select new contemporary French artists they thought she would admire. The headboards for the beds, finally, were our personal interpretation of the Negresco. We thought they would make for a nice link between the past and the future. Another link is the use of bright colors. We selected a palette inspired by the past, in particular Louis XIV, Louis XV and Empire. People used so much color in the past, wonderful green emeralds, carmine reds – colors like that can still change the atmosphere in a room. That being said, you have to be modern when you design a space, work with new materials and new technologies. I guess in the end the way we design an interior is a lot like cooking. We take a classical dish, study it very carefully, do a modern interpretation that tells a modern story – and takes it easy on the butter and cream.

Take the most important lessons of the past and make them modern in a creative way – that is one of the most important interior-designs lessons Marc learned at the prestigious École Boulle in Paris. Jeanne Augier applied it perfectly in the lobby of the hotel that became her life's work.

Decorating your home symmetrically can be a yawn-inducing affair. Over here though, the overpowering combination of turquoise-colored Chinese vases, a gold Louis XVI side table and pink-striped carpeting is more than enough to attract anyone's attention. One final piece of advice: always make sure that you have something of interest opposite a mirror.

Madame Augier asked her friend, the artist Yvaral, to custom-design the striped carpeting for the Negresco. At the time, it must have cost an arm and a leg to create the stunning print. But did you know that nowadays printing your own carpet is a lot more affordable than you'd think? Ask a young graphic designer to help you out with the design, don't be afraid to go overboard and prepare to be 'floored' by your new carpeting.

The headboards for the beds in the rooms that Marc and Nicolas designed for the Negresco are their personal interpretation of this unique hotel.

Living in a Material World

Surprising Materials
Anne van der Zwaag

When you think about materials in interior design, you can do so quite literally: what sort of fabrics do you need, which tile would be best for the bathroom. However, you can also use a different approach and ponder the history, rituals and art that went into making them. That is what I hoped to talk about with curator extraordinaire Anne van der Zwaag I had been a fan of Anne's work ever since I started visiting her ground-breaking Object Rotterdam exhibitions that showcase the newest and bestest Dutch design in highly visible and easily accessible urban locations. To my great surprise, Anne opened the door to her stately nineteenth-century town house wearing a brightly-colored African dress. It was a remarkable moment that kicked off not just an extraordinary day, but an entire month in which I visited three designers Anne suggested I meet up with. Long story short: if you want to leave all those boring mainstream materials behind you, yet still want your home to look sophisticated, then sit down and take the time to read this chapter.

What matters most is the story behind the materials, where they come from and who made them.

A finely woven *'ie toga* mat from Western Samoa serves as a reminder of Anne's exotic upbringing – and yes, it goes perfectly fine with an authentic Bavarian cuckoo clock!

Oh no, Anne forgot to impregnate the leather when she bought this Pastoe LL04 lounge chair. Her family's fingerprints – which can never, *ever* be removed – turn it into a unique design item!

The daughter of The Von

First things first, could you please tell me why are you wearing this beautiful African dress?

It's because I was born there. At the time, my father had just graduated as a veterinary scientist. He wanted to teach people living in remote regions how to become self-supporting. He was already quite well-traveled when he met my mother, who worked for the Royal Dutch Meteorological Institute. After they got married and had my brother, my father got an assignment in Cameroon, of all places. But after my parents arrived in Yaoundé, the capital, they found out that my father's assignment had been canceled at the very last moment. Instead, they were told to meet a doctor Eppo in Jakiri, a remote village in the far north of Cameroon. When my mom and dad arrived after a ten-hour trip, they were greeted not only by Dr. Eppo himself but also by just about everyone in town. They moved into this white colonial-style house at the end of a long winding path. It was called Journey's End – what a beautiful name, right? My dad started out on his assignment, my mother started teaching English and about a year later, I was born in a nearby town called Shisong. They had a Dutch doctor working there at the time.

What a coincidence!

Yes, it turned out there were quite a lot of Dutch expats working in northern Cameroon. It was a huge area, but we always knew how to reach each other. I was also baptized there by a local tribal leader called The Von. It was a three-day ceremony during which several animals were ritually slaughtered. Imagine that! My parents still have the skulls at their farm in Friesland. Now The Von was not just any old tribal leader. With the exception of his wives, no other woman was allowed to speak to him. But because I was born with white hair and a very fair skin, The Von decided that I was so unique that my mother would be allowed to present her baby to him. He baptized me and gave me my African name Jevon, which means 'daughter of The Von'. Rituals still play an important role in my life. And all the colors, the scents and the materials in Africa really have made me who I am today.

Tempus fugit! Anne saved her original school bag from Cameroon and combined it with two pillows with a mold culture print by Lizan Freijsen.

Casa Tropica

Sadly, my father's assignment in Cameroon ended after a few years and our family had to move back to the Netherlands. We stayed at Casa Tropica for a while, which was this huge villa. People from all over the world stayed at Casa Tropica and so you can imagine it was a unique place. My father took on a new assignment in Western Samoa to start a veterinary school., a place that is about as remote as it gets. And just like in Cameroon, rituals continued to make a big impression on me. Western Samoans tattoo their sons from the waist down when they reach manhood. I used to sit on the beach with the other children and watch how the freshly tattooed young men would ritually wash themselves clean in the ocean. Because Western Samoa was so remote, very little could be imported and so everyone used local materials for just about everything you can imagine. To this day, I have a papyrus mat in our son's room that we took with us when we left. When you're traveling, you should always be on the lookout for materials you can't find at home.

An unusual education

After Western Samoa, we spent a few months on Sulawesi and then on Sri Lanka. When we finally got back to the Netherlands, my brother and I spoke this weird mishmash of different languages. And so my parents sent us to a Waldorf school so that we could integrate in Dutch culture yet still be free. It was a very atypical education with lots of space for creativity and different cultures. Our subjects included astrology, mythology and mineralogy – definitely not things you would learn at a regular school but for me it was just perfect. It truly was a place where outsiders could come together. After the Waldorf school, I decided I wanted to go to a regular secondary school. I wanted to discover what it would be like to be part of 'the system' and learn regular subjects and get grades for my work. In retrospect, it was a good choice. In life, you don't only need creativity, inspiration and conceptual thinking. If you want to succeed, you also need theory and structure. I ended up studying art history. It was totally me and so I became very driven. I really immersed myself in it and learned all about the history of how humanity expressed itself visually and materially. If I now look at new developments in art, architecture, fashion and material design now, I instantly know if something is genuinely new or not. At one point my teacher said: "If you really want to do something special, you should go to the university library and see if you can recover some lost art and material-archive books." He told me that they were collected in the sixties and seventies by Frans Haks and Carel Blotkamp, who wanted to teach, not with regular books but rather with actual materials that were used by the artists themselves. I ended up spending two years recovering everything. It was an overwhelming project but also an amazing experience.

I am trying to imagine what these material-archive books look like!

Andy Warhol, for instance published *Aspen Magazine*, which was basically a box filled with all kinds of materials: cassette tapes, rolls of film, stickers... I loved how revolutionary art was at the time and all the creative disciplines started to mix: design, art, fashion, architecture, photography.

Material plays an important role in Anne's home. Heck, even some of the plants are made of felt. This particular black alocasia was made by Dutch designer duo Wandschappen.

More than meets the eye

What do you like about organizing exhibitions? If it's about an urge to show other people what beauty is to you, then you and I have something in common!

Everything comes together for me when I organize an exhibition. I enjoy the idealism that goes with it, providing young designers a podium to showcase their work and inspiring my audience to look at things from a different perspective. But I have to say that I also enjoy the entrepreneurial side. I'm not afraid to work commercially. After all, who wants to end up with a few good ideas that never find an audience? And finally, when I look back on how we lived in Cameroon and on Western Samoa, I realize that everything in life revolves about doing things together.

In the end it's not just about beautiful things?

No, design is about more than meets the eye. It can show you the thought process of a designer. Good design can also convey an emotional meaning, much like the rituals I grew up with. All the items I have here at home have a story to them. I didn't just buy them because I liked the way they looked. I see a house as a place where every aspect of your life comes together. I don't believe in homes that are decorated with only new things – they don't have any meaning to them. When I walk around my own home, I relive the moments that are connected to the things I have.

You have so many unique design pieces here – but then again you have the financial means. And let's not forget you know just about everyone who is anyone in Dutch design.

Let me tell you, everything you see here didn't just fall into my lap. I had to work very hard and build my own network from scratch. I organize my own exhibitions from the bottom up and I am convinced that anyone can do it. I see so many people around me achieve wonderful things all by themselves. Don't ever think you can't do something great.

This *V.O.W Nº45 Temporary Trees – Poplar* light box by Raw Color and Mkgk adds a playful touch to Anne's dining room.

Ask a designer

You can apply that way of thinking to your own interior as well. Take the daybed I have on my rooftop terrace. I'm sure you could buy one at a regular furniture store. But you can also find a young designer at a local graduation show and ask him or her to design something for you. You'll end up with a unique piece of design with a great story and that will last you a lifetime. And don't ever be afraid that a designer is going to say no. For many designers, it's infinitely more interesting to say they have custom-made something for a client than to tell their friends their work is sold at a concept store along with hundreds of other design pieces. And before I forget – working with a young designer can be a beautiful process that teaches you all about form and function. It helps you develop your sense of taste.

The sponge

Do you think it is possible to acquire good taste or is that something you simply either have or don't?

People sometimes say to me: "Oh, it's easy for you to say, you have such great taste!" But you know what? It took me years to develop. One of the most valuable lessons I learned from my mentor Frans Haks was to go through life like a sponge. I soak up everything I see when I go to a museum, a design exhibition or a graduation show. And then from time to time my sponge gets so full that I need to wring it out and then everything falls into place. Traveling, by the way, is also a great way to develop a sense for colors and materials. Developing good taste is a matter of seeing both beauty and ugliness.

This African club chair has been in the family ever since Anne's parents lived in Cameroon. Don't throw away things too quickly, is Anne's sage advice. A sheepskin rug not only adds some softness, but also greatly improves a room's acoustics.

Finally, another way to give meaning to your interior is to not throw away things too quickly. Try to trade with friends and family. I love to rummage in the basement of my parents' farm and discover things they've forgotten about. I am positively hooked on flea markets and secondhand stores. You can find some truly unique items there, especially outside the big cities.

You can make a tried-and-true Eames Plastic Armchair RAR look exciting and new again if you combine it with work by today's designers – like a crystal vase by Isaac Monté. If you look carefully, you can make out Anne's mother proudly presenting her baby to The Von in the framed photo next to it.

Fa-fa-fa-fa-fashion! Do you have a particularly striking item of clothing at home? Well then, it simply has to come out of the closet and become a loud and proud addition to your interior – like this striped dress by Jan Taminiau.

De tiid hâldt gjin skoft

So, money doesn't matter in the end?

You know what? It doesn't. Like many people in Africa, I prefer to live in the moment and enjoy the small successes that I have each day. Sometimes I think to myself, what if I had 100,000 euro to spend on a piece of art? Would I feel better? In the end, the only thing that matters is that you take the time to develop a sense of aesthetics. If you have it, you can find beauty no matter where you look. That is exactly why I want to keep the exhibitions I organize as accessible as possible. I like to amaze, surprise, inspire – things that are virtually impossible when you only work for the art incrowd. They've seen everything ten times over. Of course, I want them to like what I do. But what pleases me no end is when someone who is not normally interested in design walks up to me and says a whole new world has opened up for them. As a consumer, you no longer need to rely solely on galleries and museums to find visual and material inspiration. I don't think we half realize the influence social networks will have on our lives.

What else do you see happening around you?

A few years ago, everyone started developing these ultramodern new materials. But how many times have you seen anything really innovative? It all remains stuck in an experiment or a transparent acrylic cube with a piece of wood in it. What matters most is the story behind the materials, where they come from and who made them. I see more and more people around me who are starting to look for something more meaningful than the latest innovation on the market. Another important aspect in our zeitgeist is the idea of time. In today's world, we can make or change everything – except for one thing: Time never stands still. Or as they say in my Frisia where my parents live: "De tiid hâldt gjin skoft". How you spend your time and with whom is becoming more and more relevant. People nowadays are more conscious of their time and are starting to appreciate places where time passes slowly, like home.

This VW01 chair by Vouwwow is made from a single piece of honeycomb cardboard, a strong and lightweight material. And check out that multicolored bedspread by Fransje Killaars!

SURPRISING MATERIALS

Ask a young designer to make something for you. Anne did just that and she ended up with an experimental piece by Simone Post.

Do you live in an old home? You can lay bare the history of its previous inhabitants by stripping away the layers of paint on the staircase, like Anne did in her own townhouse.

Anne van der Zwaag Recommends

Simone Post

When I asked Anne van der Zwaag to pick three of her favorite Dutch designers for me to interview, I was already hoping Simone Post would be on her list. I first met Simone at the 2015 Eindhoven Design Academy graduation show. She was proud as a peacock as she stood in front of the Recycled carpet she had designed for Vlisco. It was one of the projects everyone was talking about – and not without reason. Simone's carpet struck just the right chord. It had a great story to it and looked stunning to boot. Since her graduation, Simone has been working on some exciting projects that revolve around the development of new materials. Luckily for me, it turned out that Simone lives in the same Rotterdam neighborhood as I do. And so, I hopped on my bike to shoot the breeze with one of the rising stars in Dutch design.

'I first got interested in material design through my mother. Together, we would go on day trips to museums and see exhibitions by fashion designers such as Viktor & Rolf or Hussein Chalayan. The work of these designers focused on material experiments – and I got totally into it', Simone explains. When it came to designing an actual collection, however, she quickly lost interest. Instead, Simone much preferred to focus on that first experimental material design stage – that was her true passion. 'When I switched to the Eindhoven Design Academy, it was bullseye!'

A stack of Simone's early samples on the left and the final version of the Vlisco Recycled rug on the right – it's more affordable than you'd think!

Simone's big breakthrough came during an internship at Vlisco, a company that produces fabrics that are very popular in Africa. 'Because their products are high-end, all misprints had to be destroyed,' Simone says. 'I decided to take these misprints and turn them into something new. One of the conditions was that the prints could not be recognizable. After a lot of experimentation, I ended up with a carpet that still has recognizable Vlisco colors but a totally different look.' As Simone tells me about her project, I cannot help but wonder how much work must have gone into the first prototype. Surely she must have thought to herself, 'You know what? I'll just stick to a place mat and call it a day'? Fortunately, Simone asked all her friends and family to help out in the weeks leading up to her graduation. Luckily for her, all that hard work paid off as the Vlisco Recycled Carpet turned into a runaway hit. 'The Design Academy graduation show is the perfect way for consumers and design lovers to find out what ideas and materials future designers will be working with', Simone explains.

After her graduation, Simone decided to stay at Vlisco a bit longer and work as a pattern designer. Smart move! But what does an average day look like for a pattern designer? 'As a pattern designer, you get one month to come up with a new pattern that is both new and recognizably Vlisco at the same time. I start by doing research in the archives. The next phase is to start with simple black-and-white drawings to flesh out new ideas into full compositions. The colorways usually come last. My first print featured Dutch bicycles. After that, I did one with planets that became a bit of a surprise hit in Africa.' Unfortunately, Simone hasn't had an opportunity yet to witness her African success with her own eyes. During a recent trip to Paris, however, she did come across one of her patterns. Simone loves to sniff out original items when she goes shopping in a big city, and so she found herself in one of the many African shops in Château Rouge and found her own design. 'When I showed one of the shop owners a photo of a sketch of my bicycle print, he was amazed that a Dutch woman was behind one of the prints in his shop. He even asked me if I could use a drawing of his shop in one of my new designs.'

Bold colors, clean lines. Yup, even a relatively small bedroom can still look smashing! By the way, the vase on the nightstand is by Foekje Fleur.

Another project worth checking out if you want to learn more about materials in design is Envisions. This group project, of which Simone is a part, lays bare the thought process that goes into designing new materials and products. You can see their work during Dutch Design Week or the Salone del Mobile. For companies, Envisions is the perfect place to start if they want to develop new materials, shapes and concepts for upcoming collections. Unlike many other designers, they don't develop full prototypes and then try to sell them as such. According to Simone, that would be a serious waste of everyone's time. One last word of advice from Simone: 'Contemplate where all the materials that make up the items in your home come from – it will make you appreciate them even more.'

Notice how Simone cleverly uses the same flooring in every room – it makes your place look so much bigger!

Anne van der Zwaag Recommends

Beatrice Waanders

If you're in for a feel-good story about a successful career change and want to learn about the many advantages of wool, then this story is just what you need. Let's go on a trip to The Soft World, where its main inhabitant, Beatrice Waanders, uses her personal touch to transform sheep's wool into acoustic panels and even curtains.

This story starts out with a little girl from the countryside who used to sit in her little pink room creating imaginary fashion collections and magazines for all her aunts to admire. Good interior design is nothing more than creating your own little world – it's a lesson that Beatrice learned at an unusually young age. She was lucky enough to find a very comfortable job designing the interiors of embassies and chancelleries for the Dutch Ministry of Foreign Affairs. It was very important they all had a 'Dutch' feel to them, so heaven forbid things got too shiny or ornate. Beatrice hates to admit it when we meet up, but she always bent the rules juuust a little bit to get the result she wanted.

Asked about her favorite project, Beatrice smiles and tells me it was the interior she designed for the Dutch chancellery overlooking St. Peter's Square in Vatican City – a calm and quiet last post for ambassadors that requires a hell of a lot less work than in Africa or at one of the big posts in Washington or Paris. 'The Dutch chancellery featured an interior that was painted in these soft classical colors like salmon pink and lavender blue', Beatrice explains. 'It also had these enormous medieval paintings and even a 2,500-pound pastel Murano chandelier.' She used them as inspiration for the rugs and fabrics she ended up choosing. They were made from the finest Italian satins and Rubelli velvet – luxurious materials last a lifetime! Beatrice even had an antique sofa reupholstered in alternating beige and pink stripes. Definitely a choice that is not for the faint of heart, I think, before my mind drifts off, wondering what life as a globetrotting ambassador would be like. Apparently, there are some authentic Foreign Affairs families out there with children who grow up some place else every four years.

Beatrice Waanders' wool hangings and curtains are great if you want to improve the acoustics in a room.

'When I worked in Rome, the embassy chauffeur used to drive me around the city and park his car right next to the Trevi Fountain so that I could have a drink on the terrace next to it – that diplomatic license plate came in pretty handy.' Well, well, well! But surely, you would never want to leave a cushy job like that? Unfortunately, Beatrice was let go after the Ministry had to make some long overdue budget cuts after 9/11. 'Looking back, it was a blessing in disguise', she explains. 'I wanted to do something completely different and I enrolled in as many different classes as I could. One of them was an obscure felting course in an attic in Rotterdam and I was instantly hooked. After my first day, I felted until three in the morning!'

Unlike other fabrics, felt is not woven. To Beatrice, felt is like sculpting with wool. It enables her to see every fingerprint as she pours water on it and feels how the fibers start to hook together. Beatrice works with wool from many different sheep breeds – even those that are considered too difficult to felt. Working with what's on hand, that's what Beatrice loves best. 'I never shy away from experimenting and I was surprised when I tried whether wool curtains would work. To my great surprise, they did. Who would have thought wool would look so nice with all that backlight? The curls look different at every moment of the day. I love my curtains best at sunset, when a small breeze moves them ever so gently.'

This spirit of experimentation enabled Beatrice to build up a wide collection of interior design items that the world can order online. But what about bespoke design? No problem! 'At the moment, I'm making three acoustic panels for a client in London', she explains. 'Felt and wool are excellent materials if you want to improve the acoustic quality of a room. It's a mistake people make a lot. They use hard materials on the floor, limit the amount of textile they use in a space and then complain about the horrible acoustics. My curtains and wool hangings can solve that in a heartbeat.' Sounds interesting, I think, as I notice how I've been stroking the fur I've been sitting on during my interview with Beatrice. 'Wool is very tactile. Some parents even let their baby sleep on sheep's wool. You don't have to worry about wool getting dirty. It's also a lot easier to clean than you would think. In fact, wool contains lanoline, which basically makes it self-cleaning. What matters most, in the end, is the feeling of having an actual live piece of nature at home. The Soft World is very soothing, don't you think?'

Counting sheep! Can you count how many different sheep contributed wool to this wool hanging in Beatrice's dining room?

Anne van der Zwaag Recommends

Isaac Monté

Love it or hate it – you have to agree that Isaac Monté's work provokes an emotional response. In his workshop, this Belgian designer takes unusual materials and manipulates them into unique pieces that oscillate between art and design.

A soft-spoken, all-round nice guy. That's how I would describe Isaac. His work, however, couldn't be more different. It can be pretty extreme. Isaac hasn't always been so out there, he admits. He grew up in the Flemish countryside and got his creative start working in his mother's sewing factory. 'I'd go there sometimes to sew clothes for my dolls behind one of those big industrial sewing machines', Isaac tells me with a big smile on his face. It's obviously a memory he is very fond of – even though times weren't easy since a lot of sewing work in the fashion industry started to move to low-wage countries at the time. 'My parents weren't exactly pleased when they found a letter on their doormat from the Royal Academy of Fine Arts in Antwerp confirming my application for the Fashion Design program.' Luckily for them, the grueling two-day application process turned out to be a bit too intimidating for a 17-year-old country boy with a meager portfolio. And so, Isaac decided to study interior design followed by product design instead.

'Leave your comfort zone', Isaac's teachers told him. Being the eager beaver that he is, Isaac totally went for it. He even started scraping dead cats from the streets! Isaac skinned and tanned them himself and turned them into a series of masks. For his graduation project, Isaac made bird's nests out of a material that he had created from cigarette butts that he had melted and then put into a blender until they got the right degree of fluffiness. As a follow-up project, Isaac asked his local supermarket if he could have the bacon strips that were past their sell-by date. Being the maverick that he is, Isaac turned this unusual material into a series of lampshades and vases. His more recent work is a tad more mainstream. But why? 'I realized that if I wanted to sell more work, I needed to consider other options as well.' Focus, that's what Isaac needed. And he found it – in crystal, a material that requires very particular circumstances and a lot of time to grow in nature. Isaac, however, beat nature and developed a process for crystals to grow at a highly accelerated speed.

A true interior-design aficionado is never afraid to play with materials – just imagine how stunning Isaac Monté's crystal lamp would look at your place.

'Being able to speed up time is a concept that has been on my mind lately. In our world, time has become the ultimate luxury product – no matter how rich or poor you are.' That all sounds fine and dandy, but what if you were an average consumer with some money to spend? Could you just send Isaac an email and ask if he could make something for you? The answer is: DEFINITELY! Case in point: Isaac recently received a request to design a bookcase for a client who had travelled a lot and needed a place to display his photo books. 'I ended up designing a coffee table instead. I figured his books needed to be out in the open so that you could flip through them. Be prepared to ask yourself what you really want when you work with someone like me. What I make is art with a function. Wait, let me rephrase that. Art always has a function, of course. What I mean is that my work is art with a practical function.' Well, okay! But surely good art and design can cost an arm and a leg? Hmm … no!

You can buy one of Isaac's crystal vases for as little as 50 euros. And even at that price, they are truly one of a kind. Isaac even sold two of them to a hotel designer who lives on New York City's Fifth Avenue. 'She put them in front of a painting that had the same shades of green and orange as my vases. Which goes to show you, combining expensive items with more affordable ones can have interesting results.' Thanks for the advice, Isaac! Do you have other recommendations? 'I did a crowdfunding campaign a while ago that worked like crazy. For a growing number of designers, crowdfunding is an easy and affordable way for people to get in touch with young designers and to buy original work that doesn't break the bank. However, if you do have some serious money to spend, ask for an artist's proof. It's usually a material experiment done by the artist that was part of the creation process of a finished product.'

Isaac made these vases from recycled strips of bacon. They are definitely conversation starters!

To Be Frank, You Have to Be a Rebel

Colors off the Chart
Frank Visser

He is one of Europe's best interior stylists. His work has been published in major magazines around the world. And yet, Frank Visser doesn't care one iota what his own place looks like. 'When one of my interns dropped by unexpectedly a while ago, she let out an audible, Hmm.' Frank wanted to spare me the disappointment and invited me to come to his countryside studio instead. We spent a marvelous day together as he told me tales of magazines gone by and decided to share his most precious color tips for the very first time. It was a stark reminder that true interior styling is an art form that goes far beyond everything you see on Instagram or Pinterest. You can paint by the numbers if you want a room to look halfway decent. But to be Frank, you have to be a rebel. That is the only way to make a room look colorful and sophisticated at the same time.

I always think up a story first and then find the color combinations that go with it.

Frank likes to mix in sand with his paint. It makes the colors so much livelier.

NEXT PAGE Sew together your old English college shawls and, hey presto, you have enough color inspiration to fill an entire room.

Our man in Iran

We meet at last, Mr. Visser! You've just returned from Iran, I understand?

Yes, Iran is a wonderful travel destination. It not only has some of the friendliest people you'll ever meet but you can also buy some truly unusual items on its many markets, stuff you won't find anywhere else. I found these great handmade washcloths that almost have a high-end Japanese denim feel to them. I'm sure they will end up as part of a photoshoot at one point.

Why didn't you want to meet at your home in Amsterdam?

My place looks like a total mess. I dolled it up once for a photoshoot and it looked nice for a while, admittedly, but that was it, really.

What a surprise for such a good stylist!

I'm at my best when these three things happen. First, I need a tight deadline. Second, I like the challenge of a limited budget. And then, most importantly, the place I design has to be temporary. That's all I need. Just travel the world, design and photograph something temporary and then never look back. The first time I actually did that was in Shanghai. Xu Wang, the legendary editor who had just launched *Elle Decoration* China at the time, invited me to come over and work with her for a while. She helped me find a temporary apartment that I decorated with nothing more than a few sheets of paper on the wall. We ended up doing a photoshoot there and the result was published all over the world. After that, I traveled to Mumbai and performed the same trick. I struck up a conversation with a seamstress I had met on the street and before I knew it, she had suggested I rent her place for a while.

I never would have thought you can paint a lampshade – but now that I've seen how Frank does it, I can't wait to try it at home. How about you?

Sunset on Curaçao

When did your wanderlust begin?

When I was very little, my parents and I moved to the Caribbean island of Curaçao. To me it was the most normal thing in the world, but looking back I didn't have your typical childhood. We would travel the region whenever we could. We'd go on cruises or fly to Guatemala or Mexico. Once we went hiking through the mountains of Colombia and that's when I first experienced coldness and the crackling of the fireplace in our cabin. Traveling shaped my character. It also helped me develop my own visual language.

What are your warmest memories of Curaçao?

Sunset on Curaçao is very particular. The sun goes down very quickly and right before it does, all the birds tweet one last time and then everything goes dark. I really missed that when we moved back to the Netherlands right after my twelfth birthday.

That must have been odd for all of you!

I went to secondary school and didn't give it much thought. After I graduated, I studied medicine for a while because I figured I could travel a lot as a doctor. But since I didn't care for medicine at all, I failed miserably. To make matters even worse, my parents decided to move abroad again. Right before they left, they bought me a tiny seventeenth-century townhouse on Bethaniënstraat in the heart of Amsterdam. Instead of studying, I would spend all my time exploring the city and buying clothes, which is how I landed my first job as a store-window decorator. I loved that job so much, I decided to abandon my medical career and switch to the Rietveld Academy instead to become an artist. Finally, I was no longer a lazy student – I felt unstoppable, I was so ambitious.

Trompe l'oeil reigned supreme

What did your place look like?

It was one of those typical long and narrow Amsterdam houses the Dutch like to refer to as a *pijpenla*, a pipe drawer. I would throw these elaborate dinner parties for my friends there. For decoration, I would dip a curtain in plaster, drape it over the mantle and decorate it with grapes I made out of clay. After all, it was the 1980s and *trompe l'oeil* reigned supreme. I first realized what color could do when I went through a bit of a maritime phase and painted one of the other rooms in blue. My best friend Mirjam was a budding photographer. We decided to do a photoshoot for a laugh and send it to the Dutch edition of *Elle Decoration*. It took us three long days to get everything just right and so we were quite surprised when they published it. We realized we were onto something and so we did another photoshoot at my sister's home. After that, we shot a home in Curaçao which was published in *World of Interiors*. You wouldn't believe how proud we were! One thing led to another, and Mirjam and I ended up traveling the globe together. We'd go to South America for months on end and do photoshoots at the most gorgeous homes we could find.

It takes balls – well, at least one – to combine pink, orange and lavender with glittery magenta.

Frank and his silly little colors

How did you find all those places? The Internet didn't exist in the early 1990s.

You definitely needed someone who could put you in touch with the right people. That's still how it works today. Through friends of friends, Mirjam and I always managed to find everything we needed. Luckily for us, practically no one from Europe would travel to Argentina or Uruguay at the time. All the major interior-design magazines published the photos we shot there. Mirjam and I were particularly popular in Italy. The early 2000s were the heyday of the magazine industry. In Italy, interior stylists like us were treated like true artists – and rightfully so. I believe interior styling is an art form that is very much underrated. Whenever I was back home, however, I could almost hear people talk behind my back. 'Oh, it's Frank and his silly little colors', they would say. 'It's the only thing he knows how to do, he must be dyslectic!' They thought it was so easy to put someone like me in a box. But I didn't care. I just flew back to Italy and made a killing cranking out these huge 16-page features week after week. I sometimes flip through all those old magazines and look back at everything I did. Mind you, things weren't always easy. Sometimes I would build a fabulous set and it would all be ruined by the furniture the advertisers wanted me to use. I'd throw up my hands in despair and think: 'How am I going to fit in all these new pieces? It's so much nicer to create an interior with old and new pieces mixed together!'

Plastic fantastic

When I look around your studio, I also see a lot of plastic items.

A lot of people think plastic is a cheap material that is beneath their dignity. But I sincerely believe it can be a thing of beauty. I developed my taste for plastic when I participated in an exchange program with Parsons in New York City. I had found this tiny apartment on Hudson Street and decorated it with Formica tables, plastic chairs and beaded necklaces I would find in Chinatown. I didn't have a car of course and had to cram everything I'd buy into taxi cabs – that sounds very Big Apple, don't you think? I much prefer to create a temporary interior and then just leave it behind when I'm done. I can make a place look expensive without actually using expensive objects. High-end design furniture that lasts a lifetime just isn't for me.

You make it sound so easy! Wasn't it hard to make things look good using plastic chairs?

You definitely have to know where to look. To this day, I adore those beige plastic stools you find in every Turkish shop here in Amsterdam or in any other big city for that matter. Did you know that most interior stylists find their best items in the most obscure corners of immigrant shops?

Even if they seem to clash at first, you can take different shades of the same color and combine them in a single space.

Drizzle Joburg

And now for the $64,000 question: how do you find just the right combination of colors?

Color is a great way to visualize a feeling, an atmosphere. I always think up a story first and then find the color combinations that go with it. I find them in images that visualize the story I'm telling or the atmosphere I want to create. If you want to learn how paint colors work, look up the Itten color wheel online. Teach yourself how to mix every color using nothing more than yellow, blue, red, black and white paint. Once you've mastered that, you can move on to extracting the five or eight most important colors from an image you like. It doesn't matter if you find that image online, in a magazine or in a thrift shop. Of course, you can also use one of your own photos. Whenever I'm traveling nowadays, I find it important to take my own photos. I try to find atmospheres that touch me, like the one I found in Johannesburg a while ago. It was quite rainy when I was there and so I made a series of street photographs that focused on umbrellas and all their different colors. I ended up calling it Drizzle Joburg and it gave me some great ideas for new color combinations that I may or may not end up using for an interior.

Create color connections

A rainy day in Johannesburg sounds quite coincidental. How do you plan for something like that?

You don't. Allow yourself some time and some freedom if you want to create something new. Just let things happen and take lots of photos to remember every place you've been to. You can decide later on what you're going to use and what you're going to throw away. That is exactly what interior styling entails: deciding what to keep and what to leave out.

Traveling abroad? Don't forget to check out a local market for some original color inspiration. Frank bought these handmade washcloths on a recent trip to Iran and he was totally smitten.

I once read that it's a basic human need to create order out of chaos in an aesthetically pleasing way. But can anybody do so?

There's no accounting for taste. Although I suppose it's also not wrong to say that we all need guidelines. Not everything can be beautiful. If you combine black and white in an interior, for instance, the contrast can be very harsh. The same goes for black and red. If you want your colors to work at home, you have to create a connection between them.

How do you decide which colors to use in an existing space?

I often look at what is there already. When a door is already green, I just leave it as it is and go from there. You don't have to start from scratch. I believe in action and reaction. That green door might not be something you'd chose yourself. But ask yourself what would happen if you combined it with soft pink walls. That color combination would lift up the entire space.

Yves Klein Blue is one of a handful of paint colors that cannot be mixed. You won't find it at any DIY store – it is definitely a color for those among us who are not afraid to put in a little more effort.

Frank's kitchen in his studio is another great example of how he combines different shades of the same color and then adds one or two elements of surprise.

It feels good to finally pick your brain and find out how straightforward color can be!

Sometimes the solution is literally right in front of you. If you like the colors of the vintage portable radio you find in a second-hand shop, don't be afraid to use them in an interior. And don't forget to include the bright red and blue on the on and off switch. They are there for a reason so use them as accent colors. A shiny red wall wouldn't work. But a single red ceramic pot in a room painted in different shades of grey can make all the difference. It is what I call a signal element. I buy lots of them at Mevius, which is one of Amsterdam's biggest thrift stores. I'm sure you can find similar places in every big city. I recently found this fantastic bright yellow typewriter there that I'm sure will be the starting point for a great interior.

So, an accent color can lift up all the other colors in a room if I understand you correctly?

You start with colors in the same range – a family if you will. They can work together in harmony, like each other's shadows. I worked with shades of green in my studio's kitchen, for instance. I even went one step further and added some greens that almost clash. It's that element of surprise that makes a room work. You can get away with a lot if the texture of the surfaces in a room is the same. I sometimes even mix in sand with my paint, it makes the colors so much livelier. Whenever I do so, I add a shiny signal element in a totally different color. I know that sounds strange, but I know what I'm doing. If you follow my rules, you can make a room look sophisticated and still be a rebel.

Archetypal color combinations

Wait a second. I can see that green and soft pink look good together – but how is it you come up with that particular color combination and so many people don't?

It's a classic. There are many archetypal color combinations. Think of a beach with its beige sand and blue water, that's one of the most recognizable palettes you can think of. Flowers also tend to be very pleasing to the eye, which is exactly why I thought of combining an existing green door with soft pink walls. Fruit can be a source of inspiration as well. Just go to the market, buy a melon and some lychees and place them together in a bowl. You'll see that the color combination just works.

The obvious thing to do if you want to add some color contrast to a dining room would be to paint the chairs. But why not leave them white and paint the rest of the room instead? Here's the stunning result!

Frank literally has hundreds of thrift-store items in his studio
that he can mix and match to his heart's content. It is that
spirit of playful experiment that he wants to share with the
world.

A daybed with a quilt made of leftover pieces of fabric adds
a funky chic touch to Frank's studio.

Plastic fantastic! Frank found these marvelous plastic trays
at his favorite Amsterdam thrift store.

Want to add color to a room? Why not use blotting paper
for a change?

Jewels for the Home

Light Up a Room
Ana Losa Ramalho

Is your home extremely *meh* at the moment?
Well, let me lay it on the line: your interior
isn't going anywhere if you stay in like a
hermit crab. You really need to get out. Out
of your home, out of your city and yes, even
out of your country. I do it all the time and
it works like crazy. I just book a plane ticket
to a city I've never been to, grab my camera
and start snapping. I roam the streets,
always on the lookout for interesting color
combinations, shapes and patterns that I
may or may not use at home. 'The eye has
to travel', Diana Vreeland once said. In
the Portuguese city of Porto, I stumbled
upon a shop called L de Luz. It featured the
most amazing window display with lamps
from all the different eras of the twentieth
century. I love it when that happens – you're
just walking down a city street and then
bam, love at first sight. I entered the shop
and was greeted by a slightly eccentric and
bookish-looking woman called Ana Losa
Ramalho. She had so many interesting
things to tell that I decided then and there
that I just had to find out all about her
fascination with lamps. When you think of
it, they really are jewels for the home.

Time determines which
designs survive and
which ones end
up in the trash.

Ana painstakingly cleans and restores every lamp before
she sells it – which is no mean feat, as her shop has three
floors filled with lamps in all shapes and sizes.

Before and after

So, Ana, tell me a bit about yourself before we get all excited about your lamps!

Well, I was born in 1963. The Carnation Revolution here in Portugal was in 1974, a turning point in my life and in that of many other people here in Portugal. It was a big party. I remember how everybody was celebrating in the streets. There was a very clear 'before' and 'after'.

What do you remember about the 'before'?

Above all, poverty. There was practically no middle class at the time. I guess my family was the exception that proved the rule. My father was an architect and my mother a teacher. At the time, my grandparents lived with them in the same building. My grandfather was also an architect, and quite famous too. My grandmother was a writer who had fled from the Nazis in Germany.

What was it like to grow up in such an unusual family?

First of all, our house was unlike any you saw in Porto at the time. My grandfather was a strict modernist and rejected anything old or antique. Whenever some of my classmates would come over to play, they were shocked at how modern everything looked. It was all very 1970s minimalistic with space-age sofas, chairs, a white bar, lots of abstract art and an occasional nude. My grandmother was the total opposite of my grandfather. She had left Berlin in the 1930s, when it was still quite a liberal city, and ended up in Porto, a town that was extremely conservative at the time. She used to tell me that to her, it felt like going back in time a hundred years. Women didn't have many rights, they couldn't even travel without their husbands. Luckily, she became part of a group of painters, intellectuals and writers. She became a writer herself and even translated *The Diary of Anne Frank* into Portuguese. My grandparents both had a huge influence on my life. They loved each other very much, even though they were very different. My grandmother was so chaotic. She couldn't cook and was terrible at housekeeping. My grandfather, on the other hand, was extremely organized. Everything had its own place in his room. They were both firm believers in progress, however, and so no one in our family was religious. When I was 7, my parents let me decide for myself whether or not there was a god.

That's a pretty big decision to make for a 7-year-old!

Tell me about it! I ended up telling my classmates that humans had evolved from apes – and they all laughed at me. Everyone around us was very religious and even more conservative. And even though Porto was financially poor, it was a city rich in tradition. It had some wonderful local poets, writers and visionaries. The city felt so closed off from the rest of the world. That is exactly why I decided to leave for Lisbon to study anthropology. Don't ask me why, though. I mean, what 18-year-old knows what they want to do with their life anyway?

A good interior always starts with good lighting and so lamps are objects with great potential.

A regard éloigné

Was Lisbon everything you wanted it to be and more?

Definitely. There were so many new ideas in the air at the time. Anthropology gave me a new perspective on life, *a regard éloigné*. Lisbon was also where my passion for antiques began. My grandfather was horrified: how could a girl who was raised by a strict modernist end up liking old stuff? I even married an antiques dealer and moved back to Porto. I started working in his shop and developed an appreciation for lamps. After my divorce, I started my own shop with lamps from all the different decades of the twentieth century. I sell everything from art nouveau to the 1990s.

What do you find so interesting about lamps that you decided to make them your life's work?

I like to think of lamps as art objects with a function. I love exploring their every little detail. A good interior always starts with good lighting and so lamps are objects with great potential.

You have three floors filled to the brim with lamps. Where do they all come from?

Sometimes I meet people in my shop who have just inherited a rare lamp. But most of the time I buy my lamps at auctions around Europe. Prices can feel very subjective for people outside my line of business. Through the years, however, I've become very good at determining what a lamp is worth – even if I've never seen one like it before. Whenever that happens, I look at two things: the quality of the materials and the design. Iron usually isn't a very durable material for lamps. Brass tends to be better, although there are some very durable art-nouveau works by Edgar Brand that were made of iron. Of course, with materials there are always exceptions. I've bought and sold beautiful chandeliers that were made from plastic. The quality of the design also plays a big role, of course. If you look carefully, you'll see that many lamps were originally designed with a very limited number of pre-existing tubes. And then all of a sudden, things changed, with different curves and endings.

Can you spot the brutalist 1960s pendant lamp by Holm Sørensen that is one of Ana's favorites?

From Chinoiserie to Hollywood Regency – Ana sells them all.

The story behind a vintage lamp

Do you still discover lamps you've never seen before?

All the time! Art nouveau and art deco produced fewer designs so I think I've seen most of the lamps from those two eras. The design and production of lamps boomed in the 1950s and so I still discover new ones every day. The market tends to follow trends. Right now, Hollywood Regency is a trend and so, shiny brass lamps are very hot. Some of them are a bit too decadent for my taste.

What do you like best about the lamps you sell? I suppose their history can play an important role.

To me, the story behind a vintage lamp doesn't come from the life story of its previous owner. For instance, I don't care if a lamp belonged for 50 years to a mean old woman who has just died. Unlike other antiques dealers, I don't believe in the energy that comes with an object. If a lamp changes owners, it starts a new life as far as I'm concerned. You can't get too philosophical about it. I never ask where a lamp came from. The history is in the design.

Spray-on shampoo and disposable underwear

What's your favorite decade when it comes to lamps?

I love the 1950s. It was such an optimistic time that produced an abundance of new design ideas. Progress went so quickly at the time. My grandmother started to travel a lot in the 1950s. She had this spray-on shampoo and even disposable paper underwear. I have a special place in my shop for Doria lamps from that era. They were made from painted metal plates. Doria kept prices low by using every last part of them. The designs I have here feature rows of round shapes that were cut out of the metal plates. What remained was used for another series of lamps with pointed ends. I also love Emil Stejnar, even though his lamps look a lot more frivolous. They have a lot of imagination to them. I guess it must be because Emil Stejnar was a very secretive Austrian writer who was heavily into mysticism. That's the kind of design story I like. His lamps can look very sophisticated. And that's quite an accomplishment because most of their parts are acrylic. In general, I like pieces that represent a leap forward in design. I have this brutalist pendant lamp by Holm Sørensen from the 1960s that was way ahead of its time. With a little imagination, it looks like a hat.

It's all about context

I still have some trouble with the 1980s, however. I guess it must be because it was the decade I grew up in. It feels like 'my time'. To appreciate vintage design, you need some distance. Time determines which designs survive and which ones end up in the trash.

I think I know what you mean. I used to wonder in the 1980s how people would remember that decade. The 1950s, 1960s and 1970s all had such distinctive styles. To me, the 1980s were just normal at the time.

Exactly! In the end it's all about context, though. A lamp can look totally different in another interior. The color of your walls and ceilings play a huge role, for example. For my shop, I chose a dark hue because it provides a contrast with all of the lights. And as you can see, contrast works very well. When you come here to buy a vintage lamp, don't forget to bring a few photographs. I have to see which lamp fits with the furniture. A chandelier, for instance, can't be too small or too large compared to the dining room table it hangs above. Of course, you can also make a group of three smaller pendants. Choosing a lamp that matches the style of the furniture is relatively easy. But when you want to add a lamp that is totally different, I guess you have to listen to your feeling. In the end, there are no rules. It's a sensibility.

I make a point of dropping by Morentz a few times a year. After all, it is Europe's biggest dealer in high-end vintage furniture and lighting. The last time I was there, I spotted two Alvar Aalto 'Angel's Wings' A805 floor lamps. Look at the asymmetrical shape of their louvered shades and you'll understand why they earned their unusual nicknames. And don't the Angel's Wings look great with the Larissa lounge chairs by Vittorio Introini and that amazing room divider?

Five Lightbulb Moments from a Vintage Lamp Collector

Jimmy van Gent

When it comes to vintage lighting, there are collectors and there are COLLECTORS. None, however, are probably as incredibly and unabashedly hardcore as Jimmy van Gent. As the proud owner of White Rabbit Interior, Jimmy has spent these last few years building a dizzying collection of vintage lighting. Collecting is in Jimmy's blood – as a child he was smitten by all things Coca Cola. As he got older, however, he moved on to lamps he found at second-hand shops and sold at a profit after restoring them. This allowed Jimmy to slowly expand a collection that now includes some of the finest and rarest pieces on the market. All in all, he is the person to go to if you want to learn all about vintage lighting. And that is exactly why I met up with him to write down five of his most useful insider tips. I'm having a lightbulb moment! No, strike that – I'm having five of them. In any case, let's hear it for Jimmy!

1. *Make it work!*
The first thing you should do when you buy vintage lighting is check the wiring. Things may look fine and dandy from the outside, but sometimes the wires pulverize over time. And that is a risk you do not want to take at home. Replacing the wiring is not as hard as you think, although you may want to find someone who really knows the ropes, so to speak.

2. *Buy what no one likes*
I once bought a Stil Novo lamp at an estate auction. It was at a time when nobody liked that particular style and so, the auctioneers hadn't even bothered to put a price tag on it. I ended up buying it for next to nothing. The lesson here is that if you want to buy vintage designer lighting at an affordable price, you should buy it when it is still out of fashion. What also definitely helps, is that you do as much research as you can so that you can recognize a unique piece even if it's covered in dirt.

Jimmy bridged the visual distance between his Venini chandelier and his travertine table with a brass light sculpture by Roel D'Haese and a table lamp by Maison Charles.

By planning ahead, Jimmy was able to hide all the wiring of his four wall lamps. This allows the light to shine uninterruptedly on the unusual structure of the wallpaper.

3. *Plan ahead*

If you want to use wall sconces in your interior, all those loose wires can be a real deal breaker. Plan ahead and drill slots in the wall, or have a contractor do it for you. The four wall lamps I have above my credenza are all interconnected and so I only had to drill one long slot. Of course, you do have to have to decide in advance what the layout of your room is going to be. I also wouldn't go out and just buy lamps willy-nilly. Think of the exact place where you need a lamp and go shopping for that particular spot only. If you go about it that way, I'm sure you end up with a lighting plan that works. Did you know by the way that the best lamps also look great when they are switched off?

4. *Keep it in proportion*

Just like other pieces of furniture in a room, lamps need room to breathe. You should keep enough visual distance between them if you want each lamp to truly stand out. That being said, if you have a big room, don't be afraid to go big with your lamps as well. It's all about proportions. Next, make sure you keep about an arm's length between a dining room table and the chandelier above it. As you notice, I broke this rule with the Venini chandelier about my own dining room table. It is up way too high. Unfortunately, it would be next to impossible to find some more of the original glass tubes that go over the cord and then lower it. Instead, I added a Maison Charles table lamp and a Maison Jansen brass sculpture lamp to bridge the distance. After all, you don't want things to look too empty either.

5. *Tell a story*

Some of my favorite pieces at home are vintage and have a great story to them. I once bought a wall sconce that looked so unusual, I didn't know what to make of it. I don't know about you, but I had never seen a lamp that featured a combination of brass curls and a core of amethyst. It turned out to an original piece by Marc D'Haenens. Through research, I found out all sorts of interesting details about this crazy Belgian Brutalist artist. It allows me to tell a story here at home that I would never be able to tell with new pieces.

A rare table lamp reflects its lights on a brass and glass coffee table that was once designed by celebrity photographer Willy Rizzo.

Jimmy likes to think of a white rabbit as the guide in his dreams. For years, he dreamed about how he wanted to buy the ceramic painting he used to admire as a child at a nearby bird park. Now, it's his – together with a genuine Sciolari chandelier and a rare brass cactus.

You'll rarely find a Maison Jansen palm tree lamp next to a Marc D'Haenens wall sconce and a brass sculpture by Mexican artist Sergio Bustamante. And don't even get me started on the Murano ice-glass chandelier!

Love
a Little
Rummage

Finding Vintage Furniture
Babette Kulik

Madonna once offered her a job as her personal shopper – but Babette Kulik politely turned down the Queen of Pop. Instead, she would much rather stay in London to buy and sell her own vintage furniture and books, thank you very much. After all, that is what Babette and her partner Michael Selzer love best. Together with a good friend, they also recently set up shop in San Diego, California. If you're in the area, be sure to drop by and ask Babette all about her particular nose for the rarest finds. She might just share some of her best tips with you. And if you want to become as good as Babette at finding vintage furniture and books … you have to love a little rummage!

I'd rather have nothing at home than be around furniture I don't like.

If you don't know who designed a chair, it's okay for it just to be amazing – like this rare skeleton chair that would be perfect for your mother-in-law.

London's chaotic Gallery 25 is the place where many vintage furniture dealers unearth their rarest treasures. If you go there to find just the right item for your home, it helps to look very, very carefully.

Babette, take this to Christie's!

Do you remember the first item you ever sold?

Absolutely, it was a seventeenth-century book about Chinese paintings on rice paper. And I was only 13 years old. My mother, who was a widower and worked as a *couturière*, had sent me to boarding school. It was quite expensive and so from time to time she would look through all her stuff and say, 'Babette, take this to Christie's!' I was mortified the first time she asked me to sell something. I remember going there and thinking to myself, they are going to know we're poor and that I have to sell this book to pay for my school fees! Luckily, I got a good price for it and I felt exhilarated.

What was boarding school like?

It felt like I did prison for seven years. I had grown up in London with a Spanish mother and a Uruguayan father. My first language was Spanish and since my parents had sent me to the Lycée Français, my second language was French. After my father died, my mother figured I needed to develop a proper British accent and so she sent me to boarding school. Unlike the *lycée*, it was an all-girls school and that seemed to bring out the worst in everyone. The first years in particular were very hard because I was picked on. But after that I toughened up and I was the one who was the abuser, something which did actually cause me regrets. It was a defense mechanism, I guess. I was also terrible at sports. Nobody ever wanted me to be on their team. You could almost see the other girls think, God, do I *have to* have you? Being picked last did have its advantages, however. I would sometimes end up as a reserve and be sent to the library to read. It was there that I first fell in love with books.

Lady Rendlesham's dogsbody

You must have been very happy when you graduated!

After boarding school, I felt like I needed to take a year out to travel around America. It was a big mistake, because I ended up feeling I didn't want to go to university after all. When I got home, a friend of my mother's helped me land a job at the Yves Saint Laurent boutique in London. I ended up working as Lady Rendlesham's dogsbody, which was quite harsh. I used to be in tears once a week. I remember one day my hair not being right and Lady

Rendlesham said to me in her posh voice, 'If you are going to look like a washerwoman, you might as well scrub a floor!' All she did all day was smoke, drink black coffee and eat marzipans. I wanted to be just like her! As I learned more about the fashion industry, I started going in my own direction and became a personal shopper for the rich and famous.

Combine pieces from different eras and you'll acknowledge all of them! This armchair by Guglielmo Ulrich looks even better next to Ingo Maurer's Bulb Lamp from the 1970s and contemporary art by Byron Pritchard. And don't even get me started on that black-and-gold Maison Charles lamp!

Being style-obsessed is a terrible curse

Who did you work for?

I started out shopping for fashion, but then some of my clients started asking me to shop for furniture. 'Try to find me this lamp', they would ask and I always knew exactly where to find it here in London. I got that from my mother. She was obsessive-compulsive, always viewing and buying things as she took me to all the antique and furniture shops around town as well as the auction houses. That really trained my eye. Because of my upbringing and my job as a personal shopper, I became style-obsessed, which is a terrible curse. I'd rather have nothing at home than be around furniture I don't like. I bought my first piece when I was 22 years old. It was a 7.5 foot sofa from the 1970s I had seen at Gallery 25. It was completely batty, but to me it was the most sublime thing I had ever seen. The sofa looked like I wouldn't be able to afford it at all. So right after the owner told me the price, I was like, 'Goodbye!' In the following weeks, I hatched all these schemes in my head, figuring out what I could say to convince him to bring the price down. I must have been red-faced and blushing when I went back and asked if I could pay in installments. But to my great relief, the owner took pity on me and agreed. It was the beginning of a great relationship – I buy so much from David now.

An inexhaustible supply of dog clothes

I also understand that you ran a bookshop cum members club in Soho?

I did, as a matter of fact, but not until after I lost most of my savings developing a failed line of dog clothes. When I got into my 40s, I got tired of fashion. At one point, I was staying at Chateau Marmont in Los Angeles, doing some personal shopping for Marvin Gaye's daughter. I discovered this dog shop that seemed very successful and decided then and there to cut the umbilical cord, fly back to London and start designing dog clothes. Unfortunately, I only knew how to take the luxury route. I asked a very high-end Welsh knitwear company to make all my prototypes. I went through money like you wouldn't believe it. My biggest customers were Slash from Guns N' Roses and Beyoncé, but other than them, I didn't have a lot of customers. That is why Michael and I are now the proud owners of an inexhaustible supply of dog clothes.

Luckily, I had started collecting books when I was young. They helped me fund the Society Club. I had this romantic notion of bringing coffee and books together, but anyone who came into the shop knew that the two actually don't mix. Reading a book is a very personal experience, you don't want to be distracted by clinking cups. The poetry readings we organized once a week were a ball, though. We also started selling more and more books to fashion houses such as Galliano and Dior. They often use art and fashion books as a reference when designing new collections. In our current shop, I just want to deal with beautiful things and lead a more simple and authentic life.

How do you determine what you buy for Kulik Selzer? The books and furniture you sell are very particular. Obviously, you have excellent taste.

I think as we grow older, our tastes get better, stronger. We understand more because we've seen more. When Michael and I buy books, we buy as good a quality as we can find – unless it's something that is really rare. We just sold an amazing early 1950s book on Scandinavian design, for instance. It was an ex-library copy unfortunately, but as a reference book it was dynamite. Also, every time I find a nice copy of *ID&D '66*, I buy it. It is a who's who of all the interior decorators that worked in London in the 1960s. *ID&D '66* also features a lot of restaurants and bars of that period, which I find very interesting. With its bright green carpet and leather chairs, the lobby of the Dorchester Hotel looked so much better than it does now. The British were so good at mixing antiques and new furniture at the time. They would place a plastic chair next to a Louis XVI *secrétaire* and it would be an acknowledgement of both pieces. Mixing furniture from different ages just works. It makes a room more interesting. I suppose a minimal room with just a few plastic chairs can be wonderful as well, but to me it has a deadness that I don't like.

With its ebonized frame and zebra print cowhide, this French 1930s armchair looks totally titillating.

A tale of two paintings

I've always bought things because I loved them, not necessarily because I thought they would go well with something I already had at home. Everything I have at home was bought over a 30-year period. If you look carefully, you can see it is a reflection of my life story. You see changes, nuances … As time goes by, things recede into the background and then become alive again at home. I particularly love a late Victorian painting of a dead swan that used to belong to the head of Christie's. It hangs next to an ultra-slick abstract painting of a black brush mark by James Nares. The two paintings are very different but since they both have elegant curves, they go together in a strange way.

Is it possible to acquire good taste or is it something that you just have?

I rely on my gut and my eye. I think I developed my eye when I was a child and used to shop with my mother. I'm pretty sure you can train your own eye simply by seeing a lot. I don't go for what's fashionable at the moment. I just wouldn't want a shop full of Milanese furniture from the 1940s just because it's in style right now. I would want just some of it. You should definitely try and buy a piece of vintage furniture when it's not fashionable just yet. I'd never buy Jean Royère right now, for example. Don't get me wrong, I love his work. But my god, the prices have gone up. It's just hilarious, even items that are possibly attributed to him have crazy prices. We don't attribute things to designers just for the sake of it. If you can't attribute something, it's okay for it just to be amazing. Of course, you can do all the research online and find out who designed a piece. But it's equally nice to own a piece that has a little bit of mystery to it. Sometimes I think that is even better than just buying a Jacques Adnet worth tens of thousands. If you train your eye, you learn how to recognize good design even if you don't know who made it.

'I think as we grow older, our tastes get better, stronger. We understand more because we've seen more.' True that! No one under 30 would understand that this 1972 Garden Egg chair by Peter Ghyczy looks smashing next to a classical polished marble vase and a copy of Le Corbusier's *The Radiant City.*

Mix and match, that's Babette's maxim! How about we combine this bright red Pastil Chair by Eero Aarnio with a mirrored table by Jacques Adnet, an early nineteenth-century white porcelain tea service from Paris, a pair of Barovier e Toso lamps from the 1940s and an oh-so-elegant urn-shaped table lamp by Robert de Schuytener?

In the zone at home

I can imagine you don't want to tell where you buy your books and furniture, or do you?

We get them all over, I'm not joking. We go to auctions all over Europe. We have to. I also love a little rummage online. Once I'm in the zone at home, my day is gone. I'm ruined. I can spend hours trawling through garbage and then unearth the perfect item. When I put that amount of time into finding it, I don't feel guilty turning a profit. I deserve it. My biggest thing at the moment is searching on Italian or Spanish websites. The Italians in particular are amazing at sending stuff. 1stdibs.com is also a wonderful site to use. We get some fantastic customers through 1stdibs.

To me it sometimes feels like the easy way out. All the nice stuff is already there. It's not like you have to go through hundreds of pages on eBay.

I know what you mean but then again, quality and service on 1stdibs are outstanding. Dealers on 1stdibs don't want to let down their customers. If you don't have a lot of time, it's perfect for gift buying. I found a beautiful pair of vases a while ago, signed *Christian Dior 1954*. I think they were made for a charity party he did here in England. I put them up for sale on 1stdibs and ended up selling them to this young woman in Australia. She told me she had been looking on 1stdibs for ages and this was her first purchase. Much like me, she had started as a voyeur and had turned into a buyer. I felt so good.

Jacksons is another vintage furniture dealer that has Babette's seal of approval. This vintage version of Yrjö Kukkapuro's Karuselli Easy Chair is only one of the rare items on display in the gallery on Stockholm's fancy Sibyllegatan.

There are two shops in Stockholm that Babette recommends. First, there is Dusty Deco. Run by Edin Memic Kjellvertz, this shop has a mesmerizingly blue work of art as its centerpiece. And what about that Dora Maar vase by Jonathan Adler? An instant classic!

Did you know that the Swedish customer who ordered this bespoke Arne Norell sofa back in the 1970s never actually used it? There are great stories behind the best vintage furniture pieces at Dusty Deco.

You'd almost be afraid to sit down on this rare PK-31-3 sofa or its matching PK-33 stool at Jacksons. Both were designed by Poul Kjærholm – and they look great with the Hand Grenade pendant lamps by Alvar Aalto and a surprisingly (dare I say it?) kitschy ceramic horse.

NEXT PAGE The center piece in Babette's living room is a late Victorian painting of a dead swan that used to belong to the head of Christie's. It is lined by a pair of blackamoor busts that still have their original moss and grass head decoration. Babette uses the Maison Ramsay coffee table to display the books she is currently reading.

Every nook and cranny at Babette's compact London apartment is styled to perfection. This vintage brass sconce reflects its light in the zigzagged mirrored cabinet in the corner of Babette's bedroom.

As long as Babette hasn't sold this neoclassical pineapple lamp and the gilded Sagittarius Zodiac sculpture by Philippe Cherverny, it doesn't hurt to display them at home, now does it?

FINDING VINTAGE FURNITURE

Mimi must be the laziest Cavalier King Charles Spaniel in the Greater London Metropolitan Area. She spends endless days on Babette's bed, but did manage to get up a few minutes and pose for this photo.

FINDING VINTAGE FURNITURE

Clash
of
Ages

Smart Art Buying
Flore de Brantes

Where do you start if you want to buy good art? And no, I'm not thinking of a framed poster at the mall. I'm talking Art with a capital 'A' here, Art that moves you – that once-in-a-lifetime piece that makes your room. To find out the answer, let's go to rural France and meet up with one of the most original and authentic gallerists you'll ever meet: Flore de Brantes. I mean, who in their right mind would arrange for a real-life elephant for her birthday and combine an eighteenth-century tapestry with an ultramarine credenza? The mind boggles – at least mine did when I arrived at her address and realized Flore lives in a château complete with its own fruit and vegetable garden.

My ideal is to mix beautiful things from all eras.

This comfortable red velvet chair has probably been in the family for generations. Who said that everything at home has to look brand-new?

NEXT PAGE Combine some seventeenth-century tapestries with a daring twentieth-century brass table and this is what you get.

Life at the château

Flore, first things first: what's it like to live in a place like this?

We don't actually live in the château but in a house right next to it. The buildings are connected by a subterranean tunnel that in our family is known as *le métro* – very comfortable when it rains, I can tell you! Other than that, there didn't use to be a lot of ostentatious luxury here when I grew up. In fact, to me it felt positively prehistoric. You have to realize that a château like this had no central heating and was very poorly insulated. I remember going to bed at night and hoping the iron stove would keep my bedroom warm enough through the night. It often didn't and so I'd wake up freezing in the morning. Things around here have definitely changed a lot.

My father Paul had some very old-fashioned ideas – although he was a wonderful man, I hasten to add. He was the town mayor and in his free time he liked to read and take long solitary walks around the estate. Modern living was definitely not his thing. In fact, my brother and I once asked if we could have a swimming pool in the garden. But my father thought that would be positively vulgar. Cars he liked even less. When the 1973 oil crisis came about and prices at the pump went through the roof, he figured that was that. From then on, he would drive everywhere with a horse-drawn carriage. You can imagine my embarrassment when he came to pick me up from the train station and asked me to hop aboard. I always thought it was quite extraordinary for a man who seemed to be living in the nineteenth century to end up marrying this wonderfully open-minded American woman from New York City. He met my mother, who had studied at Vassar with Jackie Kennedy, at a party in Paris. She had moved to France with little more than her college French and a typewriter and had just found a job writing a column for the *International Herald Tribune*. When my parents got married, my mother gave up her career and moved into my father's château. That must have been a big culture shock. There was precious little to do in our village. Right after my eighth birthday, I was sent to a very traditional English-style boarding school. I stayed there until I turned 18. Looking back, I rather enjoyed it. I certainly had a lot more freedom than I had being stuck in a cold château. I also made a lot of new friends from all over France. One of my best friends was Laetitia, the daughter of fashion designer Jean-Louis Scherrer. I loved spending time at their home in Paris. I thought it was all so glamorous! Laetitia and I would get into so much trouble together. Like other French children of a certain background, we were expected to dress up for the monthly *rallye*, a quintessentially French party where teenagers could dance and mingle under strict adult supervision. Laetitia and I, however, found it all terribly boring and so we would sign the register at the *rallye* and then hitchhike to Paris to watch Grace Jones dance at Le Palace or Les Bains Douches.

The red dye in this antique wallpaper has faded through the years. What remains is a stunning white-and-gold backdrop that probably looks even better now than it did originally.

Why things got all mixed up

How did you get involved in the art business?

Because of my upbringing at the château, I already knew quite a lot about eighteenth-century furniture. But my grandmother, who lived in Paris, played an equally important role in my artistic upbringing. She took me to all the important exhibitions and gave me subscriptions to art magazines for my birthday. If you want children to develop an eye for aesthetics, you have to start at an early age. Her apartment was designed by Alain Demachy, one of France's most famous *décorateurs*. It was quite classical, but there was one striking modern element: a painting in the dining room called *Le Char d'Apollon* by Odilon Redon. I could spend hours looking at it. My late American aunt Nina Hyde was also a big influence. She was the fashion editor of The Washington Post and took me to see all the major fashion shows. I briefly considered a career in fashion but ended up studying art management. I was lucky enough to land an internship at Christie's in New York City. That is where I first started to appreciate contemporary art.

I think I understand now why you like to mix up antiques with contemporary art! How did you get started as a gallerist?

I used to know quite a lot of people who lived in the other châteaux in the area. Every now and then, they would need extra cash to repair the roof or something and I would help out organizing auctions and estate sales. If you do some research online, you can find some very good *ventes aux enchères* in France. My first really big client, however, was a famous American bank owner who was building a brand-new Louis XVI château for his wife in Newport, Rhode Island. I took him on a road trip through France in my old Volvo station wagon to source all the furniture. What an adventure that was!

Are those actual Maison Jansen brass palm trees? It truly doesn't matter – they look stunning, no matter who made them.

Any Louis will do

Can you tell me who it is?

I'm afraid I can't. But I can tell you that people were very impressed whenever he pulled out his checkbook and showed them his bank account number was 001. He would smoke his first cigar at 10 in the morning and then have his first cocktail. By the end of each day, his wife would have totally worn him out. 'I don't care what you buy, honey!', he would yell. 'Any Louis will do, just pick a number already!' After our trip, I flew to America to help him decorate his château. I discovered he had been sleeping in a mobile home overlooking the construction site. I guess he really wanted to keep an eye on the project.

Of all the people this multimillionaire could have hired, why did he choose an arts and antiques dealer who had just started out?

I suppose he didn't want to spend too much money – rich people don't get rich for nothing. I used the experience to open my first gallery in Paris. The Carré Rive Gauche has over 100 arts and antiques dealers in Paris and attracts quite a lot of true art lovers. It was the best place to set up shop. I started out selling antiques only but I gradually started to mix in some contemporary pieces. Many of the other dealers were horrified, they thought it was sacrilegious. Now lots of people do it. Who would want to live in a place that is totally eighteenth century? On the other hand, a completely modern interior can be a bit cold as well, I think. My ideal is to mix beautiful things from all eras. Why limit yourself to art and furniture from one era?

Things don't get stranger than this. In one of the many bedrooms of Flore's château, I stumbled across this 1804 Joseph Dufour wallpaper called *Les Voyages du Capitaine Cook*.

If you prefer a modern interpretation of the corner of Flore's château you see above, then this is how interior designer Judith van Mourik would go about it. Printing a reproduction of a classic painting and using it as wallpaper is easier than you think, by the way.

Don't buy anything for at least half a year

Do you remember which modern artists you first started selling?

I started with twentieth-century decorative arts. I remember we sold quite a few pieces by André Arbus. I also showed some abstract paintings by Pierre Soulages that looked great with all the antiques in my gallery. Works by Soulages are worth a lot more now than they were back then. I really should have held onto them a bit longer, but there you have it. If you know what you buy, art will almost always be an excellent investment. In the end, though, I'm not driven by money. I buy what I like and then cross my fingers and hope I find someone to sell it to. You have to use your intuition. Don't listen to other people.

That's easy for you to say as an art expert! I'd like to pick your brain for a while and ask you how an average person with some money to spare can develop their own intuition.

I would say, don't buy anything for at least half a year. Start going to museums. Go to art fairs. Visit galleries in your hometown. The trick is to train your eye first. Take your time to find just the right item. Don't follow trends, they are totally useless. And by all means, don't get obsessed with the profit you may or may not make a few years down the road.

Okay, let's break down what you've just said. First, which museum would you recommend going to?

I would definitely tell you to go to Naoshima, an island in Japan that is known for its many contemporary art museums. When I arrived there last year, I was still totally jet-lagged and I loved walking around at night just enjoying the architecture. The main museum, called the Chichu, was founded by Soichiro Fukutake, the owner of the Berlitz Language Schools. His wife was such a big fan of Monet that he bought her five of his water lily paintings. I love hearing all the stories behind a work of art, knowing them makes you appreciate them so much more. All the visitors had to wear soft white slippers to avoid soiling the luminous white Carrara marble floor tiles. Can you imagine? What added even more to the spirituality of this experience was that the building was underground and almost exclusively used natural light that entered through strategically placed holes in the ceiling. At home, of course, artificial lighting works work just great. If you buy a painting, make sure you adapt your light plan at home accordingly. Ask for professional advice. Light has to travel through a space like a wave. There are many nearly invisible fixtures that can accomplish just that.

The icy blue floral patterns contrast perfectly with the warm wooden floor.

Just looking

You also suggested that people visit galleries to train their eye for art. How come so many people find them intimidating?

I know what you mean, visiting an art gallery can seem a daunting experience for some people. After all, most of the time it's just you and the gallerist. But you know what, gallerists love to talk about the pieces they are showing. Who doesn't want to share what they love with as many people as possible?

I used to get the feeling that I had to buy something the moment I went through the door.

I wish everyone who went through the door would end up buying something! But that's impossible, of course. Having a nice chat with someone who visits my gallery in Brussels can really make my day. If you prefer something a little more accessible, however, there are always plenty of art fairs you can go to.

That's where I first met you – at TEFAF in Maastricht!

TEFAF is one of the best art fairs in the world, even if you just want to look. Another advantage of going to art fairs is that you find all the dealers under one roof so you don't have to travel the world to see what they are currently selling.

'Any Louis will do', the wife of one of Flore's first clients exclaimed. This Louis XIV chair may not be fashionable right now, but it will definitely make a comeback soon.

Art doesn't have to be all hoity-toity! Even Flore de Brantes has a painting of her late cocker spaniel over the fireplace.

Everybody needs a gallerist

Which galleries would you go to if you had an unlimited budget?

For French eighteenth-century pieces I would definitely recommend Galerie J. Kugel. Bellechasse 29 and Galerie Philippe Guegan are a bit more low-key but have exquisite pieces. Whenever I'm in London, I always drop by Pace Gallery, White Cube and the surrounding galleries. I always make some time to visit the National Gallery to admire Paolo Uccelo's The Battle of San Romano, which is not for sale unfortunately. In New York, David Zwirner, Sundaram Tagore, Mary Boone and Luhring Augustine blow me away without exception. The Frick Collection is also quite inspiring, needless to say. One of the most prolific twentieth-century decorative art dealers is Galerie Chastel-Maréchal. They represent some very specific artists such as Line Vautrin, who used to make the most unusual mirrors. For ceramics and porcelain, there is nobody better than Pierre Marie Giraud in Brussels. During the last edition of TEFAF, I discovered the Tomasso Brothers, two very talented sculpture dealers from Leeds. Look up these dealers online, it will really help you develop your taste for art.

Why wouldn't I go to an artist directly if I wanted to buy a work of art?

The role of a gallerist is to gently nudge the artist in the right direction and to make sure their work is shown in the right place at the right time. We also take care of a lot of the publicity. It's a long-term commitment and you can imagine that representing an artist can be a big investment. And so, if you ask me why people don't go to the artist directly, the answer is simple: all the best artists are represented by a gallery. It's natural selection. As for me, I also like showing their work in a surprising context. I love combining an eighteenth-century tapestry with an ultramarine credenza by Hervé van der Straeten, a Pablo Reinoso bench and a striped painting by Ian Davenport. At TEFAF, the other gallerists call me *la Reine du Décalé* – the Queen of Asymmetry. That is one of my interior design secrets. Nothing is ever centered in my booth. Don't stick to symmetry. Any space looks much more exciting if you place things off-center. The artists I represent all share an ageless craftsmanship that I admire. I was so proud that Ian Davenport got to do this huge mural at the Venice Biennale recently. By the way, if you want to combine a nice city trip with some excellent art viewing, then make sure you go to the Venice Biennale.

That really is the place to be if you want to see who's hot in contemporary art, isn't it?

Yes, but I like I said, you really should ignore trends in art – especially if you buy art as an investment. A long time ago, we did an exhibition about antique fire screens, not necessarily a widely-known field. For anything between 10,000 and 30,000 euros, we sold museum-quality fire screens that could make it to the Louvre or the Rijksmuseum.

I'm seeing dollar signs in my eyes now! What should I buy today?

I guess eighteenth-century furniture is not very popular at the moment, so that might be nice to invest in. Still, I'd much rather you don't take things too seriously. I threw a huge party to celebrate my birthday last weekend and shipped in an elephant to surprise all my friends. You should have seen the looks on their faces! Moments like those are what matter in the end.

Je freine des quatre fers roughly translates as 'I'm clamping down!' Flore turned this French saying into a pun about her château, which is called Le Fresne.

NEXT PAGE This very cool glass artefact became the object of my affection when I first entered Flore's fantastic French castle.

Expert Advice from

Thong Lei

They travel the globe designing mansions for the rich and famous. They inspire a small team of interior decorators and architects to reach new artistic heights. Yes, Thong Lei and Anne Noordam of Decoration Empire have got it going on from the first sketch down to the very last detail. But if you think they only use expensive art in the homes they design for their clients – or for themselves, for that matter – then you are sorely mistaken. Art, you see, comes in all sorts shapes and prices. If you want to combine your artistic purchases in a way that works, then you need to start thinking in layers. At least, that is what I recently learned from Thong when I gave me a tour of the factory that Anne and he painstakingly converted into a truly unique home.

1. *Layer affordable art with more valuable works*
My hallway features works by artists such as Jasper Johns, Antoni Tàpies and a Thai elephant. I know what you're thinking – what? I bought it for 10 euro when I was on vacation in Thailand. Everybody oohs and aahs the moment they lay eyes on it. But it's the sixteenth-century frame it's in that tricks them. It goes to show you: what is art, anyway? In the end, it all comes down to your own gut feeling. Some things you like, others you don't. It's not about who made it. And it's most certainly not about the price. You shouldn't be afraid to layer affordable art with more valuable ones. I suppose you do need an eye for aesthetics, but that is something you can develop through the years. I bet that 99 per cent of people who think about becoming an interior designer think it's about sitting in a showroom going through color charts and fabric swatches with a client, but that is not what matters most. Art is what makes the difference. It is indispensable if you want to create a meaningful interior.

Thong would never consider selling his most prized possession, a museum-quality chair by eighteenth-century Paris furniture maker Charles Cressant that was painfully restored and then reupholstered in velvet.

2. *Layer old with new*

You can also create layers with works from different eras. The perfect place to see how that works is the Paris flea market. I've found some marvelous pieces at Les Puces and have made some great friends there. Did you know that the best dealers there are often artists themselves? They have incredible taste and they sell art, furniture and decorative items from just about every century. It helps to go to a place like that and discover what you like – it's so much better than just staying at home and looking at 1stdibs. A work of art cannot stand out if it doesn't have something to stand out from. You need tension between the different works, the furniture and the decorative items you use.

A simple desk once used by an Indian clerk now serves as Thong's dining table – the perfect place to display his favorite decorative items. The stool next to it has a totally different shape, a decoration trick that makes sure that both items stand out.

The straight lines of Thong's modern Eames chair are brought out even more by the round shapes of an African statue and a dizzying abstract painting that consists of nine individual panels.

All the items on Thong's mantle underline his conviction that a true home should never look like an anonymous showroom. Layers, that is what you need.

3. *Layer works from all over the world*

Imagine the best fusion cuisine meal you've ever had. You take a bite and as you chew you realize it has different layers of taste that reveal themselves to you one by one. The best combinations are tasteful, surprising and come from more than one culture. The wooden occasional tables I have in my living room come from Paris. They definitely have a soul to them, don't you think? Are they Moroccan? Are they from 1930's Vienna? They have a sense of international mystery to them – and they stand out even more with the abstract painting I bought in Jakarta as a backdrop. Working in layers is the essence of our work at Decoration Empire. And that is why our clients like us. They may be some of the richest and most famous people in the world, but you can do the exact same thing in your home. Just turn off your TV, go out and travel. All those sponsored interior-design TV shows drive me crazy anyway. They're all so one-dimensional! The last thing you want to do, is to make your home look like an anonymous showroom.

Thong once bought these two wooden tables in Paris. What did he pay for them? Next to nothing!

Bouquets, Nature and Decay

Picking Flowers

Michael Swier

Outspoken. Enigmatic. Flamboyant.
Those are the three first things that come to
mind when I think of Michael Swier. Not
necessarily words you would associate with a
florist, but then again Michael doesn't own
your average flower shop. Together with
his former partner René, he runs Zomers,
the *non plus ultra* when it comes to luscious
flowers, avant-garde vases and jaw-dropping
home accessories. When Zomers almost
went belly-up in the early 1990s, Michael
swooped in and saved the day. What's his
secret? And how do you make sure flowers
add maximum *oomph* to any interior? Let's
find out! A word of warning before you start
reading this chapter: Michael does not
mince words.

Why not celebrate
the moment and put
a beautiful bouquet of
flowers on the table?

Entering Zomers is like stepping into an episode of the
Twilight Zone where everything is twice as stylish.

A Greek boy in Brazil

Michael, I've been an on-again off-again customer at Zomers for close to three decades now. Yikes! Isn't it weird how little I actually know about you?

I guess I'd have to start in Athens, where I was born in 1970. I was put up for adoption and so I spent the first years of my life at an orphanage. I can't deny it didn't have a big impact on my outlook in life. Luckily, my parents adopted me just after my second birthday. They were Dutch and they had already adopted my older brother Wouter in 1968. I didn't move to the Netherlands at first, however. You see, my father was an airline pilot for KLM, which is how he had met my mother, who worked as a flight attendant. But when they got married, she had to quit her job. That's how things were done back then. She was done working anyway. At the time of my adoption a couple of years later, they were stationed in Rio de Janeiro.

So, the little Greek boy grew up in Brazil with Dutch parents? Talk about unusual!

I guess so. It didn't influence me too much because I was so little. I don't remember much from that time. My father was away a lot. He was one of the youngest KLM captains to fly all the big Boeing airplanes of that era. My mother stayed at home. She had a horrible youth growing up Jewish in wartime France and so you can imagine that had quite an impact on her life – and on mine as a consequence. I inherited many of her character traits, even though she wasn't my biological mother. Isn't that weird?

In what way are you like your mother?

Like me, my mother was quite flamboyant. Her moods were all over the place. Today doctors would probably diagnose her as bipolar. Back then, she just had a sense of drama. Brazil went through a period of hyperinflation in the early 1970s and so my mother was snapping up fur coats left and right at bargain prices. That was her to a T. I remember her trying them on frantically - can you imagine doing that in the blistering Rio de Janeiro heat?

Celebrate the moment and don't be afraid to splurge on a beautiful vase – or a luxury candle holder, a scented candle or a butterfly in a bell jar!

What about your father?

My dad was away for work for weeks on end. I used to cry so hard when he had to leave. And I behaved terribly until the very minute he got back home. I magically transformed into a good little boy when I saw him again. He was so cool, calm and collected. And like many Dutch fathers at the time, he taught me to 'act normal, that's crazy enough as it is' and to 'never air the dirty laundry' – the two sayings in our language that I still hate the most. Looking back, I had this huge inner conflict. On the outside, I was supposed to act like a well-behaved little Dutch boy. But on the inside I was still Greek, with all the drama and hysteria that comes with the territory. It never dawned on me that I should bottle up my feelings. In the end, though, my father was a good man who taught me to do everything the right way.

Michael and René paint out their entire store in a different color each season. What's stopping you from doing exactly that at home?

Where on earth does Michael find these mysterious vases? Specialist stores like Zomers are so much better if you want to find something truly original that will transform your interior.

From Brazil to Belgium

What was it like moving back to Europe after Brazil?

It certainly was different. After a brief period in Het Gooi, which is a very affluent suburb east of Amsterdam, we moved to northern Belgium. I remember my dad driving this huge American car and my mother staying at home with her two fabulous Afghan windhounds, a white one and a brown one.

What an image!

Yes, everything had to look 'just so' at the time. I have some nice memories from that period. My relationship with my mother gradually got better. Also, I started regression therapy when I was 12 and I guess that helped. I learned how to deal with the fact that I was adopted, which is pretty much impossible to process.

Do you ever feel the need to go and look for your biological parents?

It's funny you should mention that. I was flipping channels last New Year's Day, still totally hung over from the previous night. And all of a sudden I saw the Athens orphanage I grew up in. Every little detail came back to me, right up to the colors of the stones. It turned out I was watching *My Name Was Kostas*, a documentary by a Dutchman who had been adopted from the same place as me. One of the most amazing things I ended up seeing was the book with all the names of the children who lived in the orphanage. As you can hear, it's a gripping saga that does very well whenever I tell it at the bar. All kidding aside, however, I love my parents and I don't blame them for anything. They did what they thought was best at the time and that was giving my brother Wouter and me new Dutch names. They loved us unconditionally, but never realized they also had to prepare us for the emotional damage adoption inevitably does to a child.

Weren't you my tour manager?

What did you do after high school?

My parents suggested I study marketing. I wasn't very passionate about it but I followed their advice anyway and graduated as quickly as I could. I had no idea what I wanted to do next. One day, my mother pointed out that there was a job opening as a tour manager. With your personality, she said, you'll get hired in a heartbeat. My job interview was over in minutes. I told them my dad was a pilot for KLM and that I wanted to travel and then bing, bang, boom, I was hired. Minor detail: I didn't have a clue as to what the job involves. I moved to Ibiza and started helping out young tourists, most of who were there on their first vacation. It turned out to be one of the most valuable periods in my life.

In what way?

Self-actualization. Finding out you're not as fancy as you think. Not being able to let others do all the hard work. Putting in an effort and falling flat on my face.

Sounds tough!

It certainly was, but it was also a lot of fun. I learned how to organize my work perfectly. Remember this was a time before we had mobile phones, before the Internet.

Vacationing in Ibiza was very exciting if you were young, and many parents would only let you go if there was someone at the resort to keep an eye out for you. I always made sure that everyone felt right at home, which is something I still strive for to this day. But I always want something in return!

Like what?

Appreciation, mostly. It's such a great feeling when you can do everything the way people had envisioned. I know it's a terrible cliché but for me, it's a true passion. To this day, I still get people here in our shop who walk up to me and ask, weren't you my tour manager? After Ibiza, I moved to Crete and started managing even bigger tour groups. I must have walked up and down that goddamned Samariá Gorge more than 50 times. I even started organizing day trips to Athens – the city I was born in, mind you.

The blackamoor Palermitan pottery head on the left has a very colorful and dramatic vibe to it – just like Michael.

I always love playing around with all the decorative items at Zomers until I find just the right combination.

Fries or flowers?

Talk about finding the missing link!

I know, it made a big impression on me when I landed there the first time. God knows why I never went back there. Unfortunately, one day I got a call from my mother. She told me she was ill and I flew back home as fast as I could. My mother always loved flowers and so I made sure a fresh bouquet was delivered to her home every other week. And then one day, a friend of mine suggested I drive all the way to Rotterdam to check out this florist called Zomers. Which to me wasn't much of a problem, because I drove this huge car at the time. Anyway, I parked outside, went in and saw René for the very first time. And I instantly knew that he was going to be my life partner and that I was going to arrange it that very day. I hung out in the city for the rest of the day and then at night I made sure I accidentally ran into him at the bar next door. That was 24 years ago. We were together for 19 of them. And even if we're no longer a couple, we're still business partners.

Why did you fall in love with René at the time?

René was – and still is – so very refined and gentle. He was very typical and I like that in a man. To me, his shop was the perfect reflection of who he was. He's so soft-spoken. Needless to say, I'm always very much in your face.

You were the perfect yin to his yang, as they say.

Definitely! After my mother passed away, I went back to Greece to pick up work again. I did decide, however, to keep in touch with René. When I heard one day that his original business partner had run off with a lot of money, I decided to come and help him out. It turned out to be quite a challenge, there were so many debts to take care of. The first thing I did was to get in touch with all our suppliers to negotiate new arrangements to pay back what we owed them. That allowed us to start from scratch, together with the money I saved from trading in my expensive car for this rickety old 2CV. Before that, René had to use his bike to deliver these huge floral arrangements to Unilever, one of the last remaining corporate clients he had left. At the shop, we started out with stuff you wouldn't look at twice now. We even hand-painted the terracotta pots we sold back then. It was a very cheap solution that worked really well. René had such amazing taste. Every morning, we drove to the flower

auction with nothing more than a small wallet holding some cash. And then at night, we'd sit down together, count the money and figure out what we were going to buy, fries or flowers. That's how we grew our company. It was a very difficult time, but looking back it was also very nice. We were together 24/7. For Christmas we pulled out all the stops, because we wanted to create something magical at our shop. That became part of our story, much like the two stray dogs I had brought with me from Greece. They were mutts and incredibly ugly – so very different from my mother's Afghan windhounds. But I didn't mind, our customers loved them and they were with us every day during the first ten years of Zomers.

Plants look even more dramatic if you throw in a Greek statue for good measure.

NEXT PAGE Trust Michael on this one: the size of a bouquet has to be proportionate to the space it's in or the table it's on.

This combination of a faceted crystal vase and a brightly-colored orchid was a bit of a recurring theme in Michael's home. It looks great next to his yellow Fornasetti incense box.

Will you just look at the size of that plant next to the vintage leather chair? It sure is big, but it looks absolutely perfect. Michael's living room wouldn't be the same without it.

Don't be afraid to go big with your flowers as well. And don't forget to combine a floral arrangement with some books and statues in different heights.

Celebrate the moment

I guess you also had a thing or two to catch up on with flowers?

I basically had to start at square one. I've learned so much about flowers through the years. They fascinate me to no end. Cut flowers are such a weird combination of nature and decay. They blossom and then they die after a short life – such a beautiful metaphor. Life is beautiful exactly because it inevitably leads to decay. As I get older myself, I've started to feel the urge to stay good-looking myself. I can't handle not staying young. But it also makes me realize I have to do something about it. If life were infinite, I wouldn't have to worry about stuff like that. And that is exactly why I think it's such a disgrace that we don't spend more on flowers. Here in Europe, we have so much to be thankful for right now.

There were flowers and plants in every single room. Heck, there was even a small bouquet in the bathroom. Talk about having an eye for detail!

We need to stop being so modest and start enjoying everything we have to the fullest. Why not celebrate the moment and put a beautiful bouquet of flowers on the table? Life is too short not to do so. This time of year, for instance, we have these peonies that look like giant balls of crepe paper. And so what if they're six euros each? Who fucking cares? They last for 12 days! You can't reduce everything to numbers. I hate when customers complain about how they've read somewhere that this or that flower should have lasted seven days but didn't. Again, who fucking cares? When you're with friends, you can finish off a good bottle of wine in minutes. Just let things be what they are, but don't forget to take good care of them.

This book has an international audience, so let's hear it for your marketing pitch!

I don't have one. Zomers is the DNA of René and me. No more, no less. If I get angry in the store, then so be it. And if you're there to witness it, I don't care. I don't have that self-control. I'm real and our flowers are real. I want to elicit a reaction with what we do. With the combinations we make, the color palettes we compose. And that goes for the entire team. We create under pressure every day. Our flowers have our moods in them, the changing of the seasons, the weather – it's all in there. Those new online florists you see popping up can never do what we do. They may raise millions, have all the customer data you'd ever need but in the end they will never be better. You can't reduce flowers to an algorithm. In the end, it's not about flowers, it's about being there for someone. Whether someone buys a bouquet for his mother's birthday or for a colleague who is ill, I find it so nice that I can create some ease of mind. Just let me take care of everything.

A single oversized branch in a tall vase is but one of several dramatic gestures in Michael's bedroom.

PICKING FLOWERS

Kitchens can be sooo boring, but not if you place a row of similar-looking vases on the cooker hood.

I bet you get some great stories from the bouquet tags you write.

Sure I do! Of course I'd never be able to pull it off, but I would have loved to publish a book about all the bouquet tags I have written. The stories behind them would have made for some very juicy reading. Sometimes customers call and ask if I can write a certain line on the tag that makes me wonder, what the hell is going on here? And then this prim and proper old lady walks in to collect the bouquet and I think to myself, now, that's not at all how I imagined you would be!

What is the most important lesson you've learned about using flowers in an interior?

First of all, the size of a bouquet has to be proportionate to the space it's in or the table it's on. I hate it when you walk into this giant living room and you see this tiny bouquet. Flowers bring a room to life. They add visual depth. Secondly, make sure that flowers become a part of the bigger story you're telling with your interior. Make sure they stand out, create contrast and add an element of surprise. And don't forget to look at every little detail. And finally, don't be afraid to spend money on some decent vases. It's all about the joy they can bring you. People aren't afraid to buy themselves expensive cars, so why not add some luxury items to your living room? You spend more time there, anyway. And don't worry if not too many people see them. Do it for yourself, create your own little moments of happiness. That being said, money doesn't create good taste. It may remove limitations, but it always takes away the effort you have to make to create something beautiful.

Go big on the balcony! A single oversized plant often looks better than several small ones.

NEXT PAGE All of the lights! Surprise your guests with a hallway that sets the tone for the rest of your home.

Slowly Moving Rocks

Feeling Zen with Trends
Candida Zanelli

If there is one woman who got me started as a true interior-design aficionado, it must be Candida Zanelli. I remember how once a month I used to go to the only place in town that sold *Elle Decor Italia* hoping its latest issue had arrived. It is almost unimaginable now, but in the early 2000s there were very few groundbreaking interiors to be found online. Like many others at the time, I depended heavily on interior-design magazines. Again and again, I would pour over the pages and analyze what turned a good interior into a jaw-droppingly fantabulous groundbreaking one. By doing so, I found out that all my favorite pages in *Elle Decor Italia* were made by one and the same woman: Candida Zanelli. I looked up Candida in her hometown of Milan to learn more about her vision, the way she looks at trends and how she navigates the overwhelming experience that is the annual Milan Design Week.

You have to take away things at home, not add them.

The warm wood of both the chair and the pendant lamp contrast beautifully with the cold, smooth surface of this amazing Perspex table.

Dreaming of Japan

It is so special to finally sit here with the woman who unwittingly started me out on my path as an interior-design aficionado.

It's funny you told me how you used to collect your favorite pages from the magazines I was in. When I was a teenager growing up Milan, I did the exact same thing. I even made them into collages about materials, food and travel. Collage can be a great method to arrange visual ideas, especially when you're thinking of a new interior. As I gradually got better at making them, I started to appreciate good design and photography. I remember we had a Japanese ceramic horse at home. I would look at it and daydream about traveling to Japan. For my parents, that was pretty much out of the question. My father was way too busy working as an army doctor in Tripoli. My mother was a housewife. Both of them were quite modern, but they didn't really know what to make of my creative streak. They didn't encourage me to become an artist. Instead, they would have preferred me to become a teacher. Art academy, they figured, was for other people. I stubbornly continued working on my drawing skills as I studied to become a teacher. After I graduated, I found a job at an animation studio preparing cartoons. Japan continued to be on my mind and I read every book about it I could lay my hands on. And then in 1974, I finally got to spend one month in Japan. I was fascinated by the contradictions of Japanese culture. Technology versus tradition, the quintessential Japanese dilemma. I decided to focus on the traditional side and to take courses in ikebana, origami and karesansui.

Scusa? Karesan-che?

Karesansui is the art of the Japanese rock garden – a miniaturized and stylized landscape, if you will. And it made me realize for the first time how styling can be an art form. I was particularly fascinated by the idea that when people started renovating abandoned gardens, they initially left the rocks right where they had found them. That left them with a challenge, because according to the principles of karesansui, the rocks should be in the center of a garden. And so, I learned that karesansui gardeners move their rocks to the center a few inches each year. You can't move them too quickly. After all, the rocks have souls that you shouldn't disturb. I am a Western woman at heart, but I am definitely drawn to the poetic nature of Japan. Like the rocks in a karesansui garden, trends that matter move slowly as well.

This space at DIMORESTUDIO in Milan might look like a showroom, but with a little imagination it's not too hard to translate its most striking elements to your own home.

Picking flowers along the Naviglio

In what other ways has Japan influenced your vision?

When I got back to Italy, I took a course in ikebana, traditional Japanese flower arranging. At the time, the Ohara School in Milan was the only recognized ikebana school in Europe, so you can imagine it was quite special. Together with the other students, we once left the city to pick flowers along the Naviglio canal. We particularly looked for irises because we often saw painted versions on Japanese folding screens. Our teacher asked us to look at the flowers very, very carefully until we could make out the tiniest parts. We would then go back to our classroom to make an arrangement in a landscape vase. The goal was to recreate from memory how we had experienced the irises in their natural environment. It was a very meditative experience that was enhanced by some very soothing Japanese music playing in the background. For four hours, we worked in total silence as we took apart every iris we had picked and then put them back together just as we had seen them along the canal.

That really must have taught you to observe things carefully!

In order to truly see the details, you have to be very calm – that goes for ikebana but also for an interior. It taught me that a composition can be very simple and extremely complex at the same time. In my work, I eliminate every superfluous detail until all that remains is what is actually needed. I know the trend right now is to add a lot of things to an interior. That is not the spirit of my work. You have to take away things at home, not add them. After ikebana, I also spent many years studying the history of Western floral arrangements to understand the differences. To me, flowers were a window I used to look at the different decorative styles from the Middle Ages up until now. If you want to understand how trends in interior design are created, you have to understand their development and their place in history first. Get a sense of which developments in society caused certain styles to go in and out of fashion again.

When you visit Milan Design Week, be sure to look carefully at the four elements of styling to discover new trends. New colors, shapes, materials and prints tell you where design is headed. The shape of a chair at DIMORESTUDIO, for instance, looks like Japanese origami – definitely a trend we'll be seeing more of.

Clean and simple lines – this ceiling lamp at DIMORESTUDIO
is the perfect embodiment of Candida's vision. By the way,
did you notice how the ceiling looks so much better painted
out in the same color as the walls? White is not always right!

I'll admit these giant silk lanterns would be hugely unpractical
in an average home. Buy them a bit smaller, however, and
bing, bang, boom, you'll have successfully applied a design
trend in your interior.

Candida loved just about everything from Sé at Rossana Orlandi – it's definitely a great place to start at Milan Design Week.

NEXT PAGE The straight lines of the artwork over the sofa provide the perfect contrast with the round lines of the different pieces in this room.

Start thinking in lines

You also organized the first exhibition in Italy about origami in the 1980s.

Yes, for many people at the time it was something totally new. Isn't it amazing that something as simple as folding a piece of paper can become such a runaway success? Akira Yoshizawa, who was one of the great modern origami masters, showed his work at our exhibition. It was so simple and modern. Origami is great if you want to start thinking in lines. It also teaches concentration and eye-hand coordination. Once a week, we also had a lecture by Bruno Munari, an artist and designer whose furniture fitted the graphic and precise nature of origami. You should look up some of the furniture Bruno Munari designed if you want to understand my vision. After having seen the exhibition, the editors of some of the biggest interior design magazines in Italy asked if I could do photoshoots about Japanese decoration. One thing led to another and before I knew it, I was asked by *Elle Decor Italia* to help them with the launch of their first issue. I worked for them for many years. It's fantastic to hear that my work for *Elle Decor Italia* inspired you so much that we're sitting here in Milan today!

Tabula rasa

Your work for Elle Decor Italia *was extremely colorful. Yet you also say that less is more. Don't you see a contradiction there?*

You can work with strong colors as long as you don't use too many. Keep it simple. That was one of the biggest lessons I had to teach when I was asked to help launch the Chinese edition of *Elle Decoration* in 2004. It was an interesting experience, I can tell you. I've also been working for *AD China* for over a decade now. The first photoshoot we did in China was total chaos. It was at the home of a French woman. She had left before the crew arrived and the house looked picture-perfect. Then all of a sudden there were six, seven, eight people there just to see what was going on. They started talking, drinking and eating, and before I knew it, there was a mess everywhere I looked. I had to throw out everyone and create some order out of chaos.

That sounds like the sound advice we could all use from time to time!

It can definitely help sometimes to completely clear out a room and start over again. *Tabula rasa!* Then, I would advise you to think of a color scheme. Again, keep it simple. Too many colors can be *confusonario*, as we say in Italian. And then finally, you start to add things – but only good quality. You have to work very slowly. Just think of my story about the Japanese rock gardens.

Don't be afraid of the dark! This bottle-green wall color makes an elegant white sofa stand out even more.

NEXT PAGE This shade of rusty orange might not be the most obvious choice for a living room, but it does have an understated elegance that makes all your furniture look even better.

The place to be in Milan

Every April, anyone who is anything in the world of interior design travels to Milan to see the Salone del Mobile. What are the best places to visit?

In general, the most interesting things during Milan Design Week don't actually happen at the Salone del Mobile itself. It is basically a fair in an exhibition center outside the city. It can get very crowded and generally I don't think it is worth your while if you want to see really innovative things. If you decide to visit Milan Design Week, it's better to stay in the city and focus on the *Fuorisalone*. Milan has multiple design districts that are each worth spending one day in: Zona Tortona, Brera, Ventura Lambrate and other new places. The 10 Corso Como concept store is also definitely worth checking out. And then every year, there are temporary locations in the most beautiful *palazzi* around town. But no matter how much changes with each edition of Milan Design Week, there is always one destination onto itself that you cannot miss: Spazio Rossana Orlandi. It is a combined exhibition space and design shop that is owned by my good friend Rossana Orlandi. You won't easily find anything like her place – or anyone like her for that matter. It is housed in an old necktie factory, one of the best known in Milan. When Rossana first set up shop, she kept all the rolls of fabric so that she could keep the history of the place intact. When you decorate a space, don't forget it has a story of its own.

Take photos with your mind

There are always so many new things to see at the Fuorisalone. *I can imagine that it can be visually overwhelming for most people. How does your eye work?*

In general, it is a good idea to focus on the four elements of styling: colors, shapes, materials and patterns. Sometimes the tiniest details can strike me. Other than that, I have to admit that I also go to Rossana Orlandi simply to look at the people, to see how they dress and to soak up the atmosphere.

When we walked around earlier, I noticed you didn't take any photos.

Unlike most people, I don't take too many photos with my phone. Instead, I take them with my mind. Weeks can pass by before I ask my assistant: 'Do you remember that

table we saw the other day at Rossana's?' It's all in my head. My advice would be: look at things like you don't have a camera with you – or even better: don't bring one at all. You'll pay much more attention to what you see.

How can people keep their homes up-to-date now that interior-design trends change at the drop of a hat?

In times like these when things around us change so quickly, it is important to stay true to yourself. You can follow short-term trends if you like but you certainly don't have to. In the end, they are just fads that come and go every season. The bigger and longer-lasting interior design trends are much more interesting. Nature, of course, has been an important trend for quite some time now. Although I sometimes wonder how we can make nature as a trend even more widespread. The environment is seen as a general problem, not an individual problem. We don't feel the consequences of our behavior yet.

I guess people don't want to change until they run out of options and really have to.

Yes, that's true. Right now, it seems very few people understand we have to adapt how we live and decorate our homes. But we really do. Don't throw out your old armchair. Just reupholster it. It's better for the environment. And it also allows you to hold onto all the nice memories that are attached to it. And if you do buy something new, make sure it is durable and will continue to look great as it ages.

Mobiles are simple, light and meditative, according to Candida. She has liked them for years, but was never able to find one. At this year's Salone del Mobile, they were just about everywhere. Take it from Candida, Milan is definitely the city where interior-design trends start out!

The Only Trend Is…That There Is No Trend

Judith van Mourik

Agrees with Candida Zanelli

If there is one person who learned how to discover trends and then chose to dutifully ignore them, it is rising hospitality designer and interior architect Judith van Mourik. As part of her study, she did an internship with Lidewij Edelkoort, the woman who is often seen as the be-all and end-all of trend forecasting. And you know what? Even though 'Li' can predict trends in just about every field imaginable, Judith advises you to just forget them. For her, the only trend is … that there is no trend. Instead, she thinks you should turn your home into the ultimate reflection of who you truly are. But how? Judith has the answers!

1. *Connect the dots … and then erase them*
These past few decades, we've all come to accept trends as a given. Colors, shapes, materials and patterns – they change every season. These past few years I've noticed that the true tastemakers among us have thrown everything overboard and started doing their own thing instead. So incredibly liberating! But ask yourself this: how did we get so caught up in the idea of trends in the first place? As a one-time intern for Li Edelkoort in Paris, I learned how to do my research in vintage art, fashion and design books and I remember the elements that captured me the most. I would then go out in the street and see if I could spot connections. Do I see the same color in a dress someone is wearing? Or a similar shape in a sofa I see? This intuitive way of finding and defining trends is what has made Li one of the most successful trend forecasters in the world. And you know what? If you look carefully wherever you go, you too can connect the dots … and then erase them.

Both Candida and Judith embrace modern technology, provided it adds something to an interior. In one of the spaces Judith decorated recently, she used a Samsung Serif designed by Ronan and Erwan Bouroullec.

2. *Contrasts and contradictions*

You can also add visual interest at home by playing with contrasts. Combine raw materials with soft and sexy ones, for example. Or mix up masculine shapes with feminine colors. I once designed a space that had a white ceiling and some very visible black loudspeakers attached to it. All that technology looked way too harsh and masculine, so I decided to paint everything in a powdery pink hue. All of a sudden, the ceiling looked extremely soft and feminine. I recently finished one of my biggest projects, the transformation of the old Dutch estate of Parc Broekhuizen into a modern hotel. The main building is quite old and it wouldn't have made sense to use furniture in the same heavy-handed Louis XVI style. Instead, I decided to create a contrast by keeping everything light and simple. That way, both the building and the furniture get the opportunity to stand out.

Talk about contrast! Put a bottle-green soft velvet stool in your bathroom and combine it with open-book marble.

Less is more! Less is a bore! There is something to be said for both. But as far as Judith and Candida are concerned, sometimes taking things away instead is what works best.

3. *The four elements*

As a student, I always wanted to design interiors that were totally new. My teachers, however, told me that total newness is an impossibility. Everything has been done before, they said. And it's true! In the 1970s, we created a luxury look at home by combining wood with the color black. Now, we do the exact same thing with wood and brass. Again, remember the four elements of styling: colors, shapes, materials and patterns. If you take a piece of furniture and change one of these elements, you can create something new at home.

4. *Put in an effort*

I know this sounds easy, but building a great interior really takes time and effort. You can't just drive to your local furniture mall and buy everything in one afternoon. If you want to find just the right wine glasses, be ready to spend years trawling through vintage markets to collect a full set. In general, it really helps if you go out as much as you can. Travel the world, get inspired by hotel interiors and examine visual ideas in art galleries and museums – that's how develop your own taste. So many people pin interior design ideas on their Pinterest boards without ever realizing an algorithm makes sure only the most mainstream images show up in their feed.

5. *How to beat Milan*

Along with tens of thousands of other interior-design professionals, I go to Milan Design Week whenever I can. And just like Candida and you, I loved DIMORESTUDIO. Even though parts of it looked like a highly conceptual showroom, you can easily translate individual colors and shapes to your own home. Here's how you find hidden gems like DIMORESTUDIO if you've never been to Milan before. Spend only one day at the fair – it's so overwhelming. I much prefer exploring the city. I usually start out at a brand I know in Brera and then just walk around the area checking out whatever I end up finding. As with many things in life, it's so much nicer to leave the beaten path and discover new things.

Don't be Captain Obvious and buy furniture from the same era your home was built in. Live in an old house? Keep it clean and simple!

Sugar, Spice and All Things Nice

The Art of Hosting

Tasha Marks

So, now that you've read how to build your own colorful and sophisticated interior, all that remains is one final question: what good is it if you don't have any friends to share it with? Invite them over, throw a party and serve delicious food and drinks with showmanship. Yes, you can be the host – or hostess – with the mostest! But where do you start? Let's go to London to find out the answer from food historian Tasha Marks, founder of AVM Curiosities – and learn a thing or two about sugar, spice and everything nice! After that, let's go back to my place! I'd love to show you how I have transformed a pretty average fourth-floor apartment into a colorful and sophisticated space. And lucky for me, my close friend and food stylist extraordinaire Alexandra Schijf is on the scene to help me out to get our party started!

Life happens over food.

Place your most unusual items in a special cabinet of curiosities like Tasha does. They look so much better if you group them together.

Food for thought

Hi Tasha! When I started telling people around me that I was going to meet up with a food historian, no one even knew there was such a thing!

Oh, I know exactly what you mean. People often ask me: 'How did you end up doing an unusual job like that?' It just seemed like the logical choice for me. I couldn't do anything else. I wasn't into history at school, but when I went to university to study Art History, I started to learn about the past through tangible things like objects and food, and for me, it all suddenly made sense. When there was a dish I could engage with, I realized that there also was a story to be told. It became less about history and more about storytelling.

Looking back, do you know how you came to that revelation?

For me it's a key part of our culture, life revolves around food, life happens over food. I grew up in Central London, where the city is a melting pot of backgrounds, identities and cuisines. Growing up here means you should be tolerant of other people and cultures; they're on your doorstep so you should participate and be respectful. My family lived in a predominantly Arabic area and so the moment I walked out onto the street, there were shisha pipes, lovely humus, spices, and other Arabic food. That was the food culture I grew up in, however my family is also Jewish, which means that food and eating have always been really important. 'We're Jews of the delicatessen, not the temple', my mother would say. We like Jewish humor and we do celebrate Passover every year. However, we also celebrate Christmas. I always joke that we are pick-and-choosy Jewsies.

I'll just pretend I didn't hear that but go on!

I didn't cook much when I was young, that was my mother's department. I remember my mum saying that, when her parents had Passover at their house, they would sit at the table double-stacked. You would sit behind

someone else and then take turns. I love that chaos around the dinner table. My mum is a really good cook and she used to cook for us – a lot. She wasn't really a baker or anything. She just made loads of food and kept a well-stocked fridge. We had a very informal house that used to attract many of my friends. They hung out there so much, my mother would start shopping for them. I would open a cupboard and ask her: 'Why are these in here? We don't like them!' And my mum would say: 'Oh, your friend Alicia likes them!' She was happiest when things weren't particularly formal or structured. Everyone could just eat whatever they wanted.

This is what I want to do

After a lost year studying psychology, I was totally focused when I was finally able to start out in art history. 'This is what I want to do!', I thought to myself. My university was partnered with the Victoria and Albert Museum and so our courses changed depending on which V & A curator was free. Had I gone straight to art history, my final-year course would have been Chinese ceramics. And you and I probably wouldn't be sitting here. But since I started a year later, it was food history. And it changed everything for me. Food is really democratic. People get involved whenever they eat. That is why food history is undergoing a resurgence now. Even five years ago, the idea of a food historian would be that of an older lady making mutton pie or something.

When Tasha got married, she decorated the dinner table with her collection of classic busts. A very chic and sophisticated solution that won't break the bank!

Petrichor and photogrammetry

Soon after you started your own business, AVM Curiosities. How would you describe what you do?

At the core, I am a storyteller who uses food history to link the past to the future. I introduce taste, smell, sound and textures into the gallery space. I once developed scent chambers at the National Gallery. One of my favorite paintings there is *Rain, Steam and Speed* by William Turner. It shows a nineteenth-century train going through the countryside, a real mix of urban and rural. I put an Edwardian tin hat box next to it. Inside there was a load of coal smothered in liquid smoke and woodchips infused with petrichor, which is the scent the earth releases after it rains. That really brought out the story of the painting. I'm also working on a Renaissance sugar sculpture workshop at the moment. I use a new process called photogrammetry that enables you to take pictures of an object and render it in 3D. I then invert it and turn it into a mold so that I can make sugar sculptures out of various items in the V & A collection.

The power of sugar

What is your favorite period in food history?

I love the Elizabethan period, that was when the dessert was born. Sugar is my passion. Sugar is not necessary. It's just a lovely addition. You can be super playful with it. Almost everybody has a sweet tooth and so you can pretty much push the boundary of what you do. Sugar first came to England in the twelfth century. It was seen as a medicine and not necessarily as a sweetener. But when sugar started to be treated as a dessert around 300 years later, it turned into a very powerful status symbol that was used to show your power, allegiances and political leanings. Sugar was still so expensive that people would only invite their top guests to stay for dessert after a banquet. In fact, there even were special banqueting houses built just to have dessert. Can you imagine a building that was meant just for dessert? I guess you can say it was a site-specific art form before people even knew what it was.

What's it like to cook a recipe from an old recipe book?

It's quite difficult to get the basics right. Recipe books used to be written for an audience that already knew what they were doing. A recipe might say: 'Mix the eggs and the sugar' – and it wouldn't specify how much you need.

If it did, it was often in older English measurements, like 'a gill of milk'. Tastes were also quite different. For centuries, sugar was treated as a spice. There wasn't a clear separation between sweet and savory and so you might add chicken to a recipe for jelly. Mince pies had not only meat in them, but also sugar and sultanas. To a modern palate they are horrible, but back then these dishes would have been a lot more acceptable.

A crossroads of ingredients

Do you also research food history in other parts of the world?

Definitely! I went on this great research trip to Turkey a while ago. I met up with rosewater experts, old confectioners and even with the inventor of popping candy. Istanbul is such a melting pot of East and West, old and new. It's also a crossroads of ingredients. There is a Turkish drink called *sharbat*, which is a tangy, half-frozen drink made with lemon. Explorers from England took a liking to it and they would powder it so that they could bring it home. That is where we got sherbets from. The technique for ice cream also originated in the Middle East, we might think of a 99 Flake as a quintessential British treat, but in Georgian Era England, ice cream was made in hundreds of flavors, more than any ice cream shop today. In the 18th century, the flavors were hugely experimental; asparagus, Parmesan, brown bread, barberries and quince are just a few that we don't see often now.

I get fat just thinking about it!

Our diets have gotten a whole lot sweeter over the years. It's high time we start treating sugar as a treat again. In itself, sugar is not evil. It's about moderation and saving it for a special occasion. Just because you can go to a corner shop and buy a chocolate bar for a pound doesn't mean you should do it every day. We live in a culture of excess in which we try to create exclusivity where there isn't any. Instead, we should use sugar to enjoy the moment. And don't forget to put some more of that historic showmanship into it.

LEFT At Leighton House in London, Tasha showed me that even a simple tray with peaches can look absolutely stunning if you present it in a colorful and sophisticated interior.

NEXT PAGE This is how you do it! Buy a high-quality white tablecloth, collect some great-looking props and present your food like a classic still life that is bound to wow your guests.

The art of hosting

Okay, let's get practical! If you want to master the art of hosting, how should you go about it?

First, you have to find out who is coming. So many people are vegetarian or vegan nowadays. It often affects what I'm cooking. If I'm having a small dinner party, I always think it's nice to ask what people love to eat. I want them to be excited about the menu. I'll leave the theater for dessert. Informal parties are the best. It also helps to prepare as much as possible in big batches in the days leading up to your party – that way you can spend as much time as you want with your guests.

Sounds great! Do you work with a theme?

No, but my wife and I do throw a cocktail party each year to fill up the dead time between Christmas and New Year's Eve. I send out a list of artisanal cocktails in advance and ask everyone to bring something. Last year, some of my most dedicated friends made a big batch of winter Aperol Spritz. They had infused the Aperol with rosemary for over a week. We even added a bit of whiskey to it to make it just that bit stronger. I also served unusual fruits after a dinner party once. I like mooching around the market or discovering new ingredients at the Turkish supermarket. I bought a snake fruit from Indonesia that tasted like a woody apple – I'd never heard of it before! My favorite fruit, however, is a granadilla, which is like a golden passion fruit. Together with my guests, we cracked open the shells and sucked out all the little seeds.

Where do you get the props for your table?

I go to antiques markets a lot. There's a good one just outside London called Kempton market. It's where all the antiques buyers get their stuff. If you go really early, you can find some great things at reasonable prices. For cooks, there is a specialist place on Portobello Road called Appleby Antiques. They have some great food molds that still have the tin lining so that you can use them. They're a bit more expensive, so I only go there as a special treat. I also have some eighteenth-century butter stamps that I use for biscuits. I just collect a lot in general. I keep my favorite items in a special cabinet of curiosities. I call myself a minimalist trapped in a collector's body. I love my possessions but you can also feel trapped by them. My aesthetics is 'sweet shop meets museum'. I often place a few jars with gobstoppers on the table because it adds a bit of color.

At our wedding, we had a table full of busts. If you want to mix old and new, it helps to add some antiques as decoration!

Parties at my place tend to spill over into the hallway, where guests are greeted by striped paintings by Ditty Ketting and the silly second-hand lamp I love to hate. Such an odd combination!

What's not to like about Maarten Wetsema's photo of a cute Pekingese dog sitting on a table? Art can be the perfect cocktail party conversation starter!

I used my trusty old brass bar cart to serve drinks in style and show off my Isaac Monté pink crystal lamp. The red Lampe Berger on the bottom shelf added a sophisticated scent during cocktail hour.

NEXT PAGE I followed Tasha to a T and arranged an informal buffet table. After all, what good is having a nice home if you don't share it with the people you love?

That's Volume

Time to unwind! I'd love to catch up on everything that's been going on. It's been a crazy year, to say the least. I traveled all over Europe and got to meet some amazing individuals. Real characters, each and every one of them. They all told me their life stories. Some of them grew up rich, others not. But money doesn't matter in the end. What all these people do have in common, however, is that they all want to express themselves with beauty. To be surrounded at home with the things that tell the story of who they are – whether it's a unique piece of furniture, a thought-provoking work of art or a stunning bouquet of flowers. The people I've met aren't afraid of taking the road less traveled. Because they instinctively know that if you want to stand out, you have to be different. Loud and proud. That's volume. Want another Campari on the rocks?

Spotify
Surprise

Spotify Surprise

Surprise! Do you ever wonder what kind of music all the people in this book listen to? Scan the barcode at the end of each playlist with the Spotify app and discover all their favorite songs.

Studio MHNA

Trois petites notes de musique
Yves Montand

Septembre
Barbara, Alexandre Tharaud, Camélia Jordana

La Bohème
Charles Aznavour

You Know I'm No Good
Amy Winehouse

We Might Be Dead by Tomorrow
Soko

Norma: "Casta Diva"
Vincenzo Bellini, Cecilia Bartoli

Parce que je t'aime
Barbara

Paradis perdus
Christine and the Queens

Merope: "Sposa, non mi conosci"
Germiniano Giacomelli, Cecilia Bartoli

If The Stars Were Mine
Melody Gardot

Tous les mêmes
Stromae

Le rempart
Vanessa Paradis

Nocturne No.1 in B Flat Minor, Op.9 No.1
Frédéric Chopin, Claudio Arrau

Ave Maria: arr. from Bach's Prelude No.1 BWV 846
Charles Gounod, Cecilia Bartoli

Les pêcheurs de perles: "Je crois entendre encore"
Georges Bizet, Joseph Calleja

Amours des feintes – Live
Jane Birkin

Les chansons des vieux amants
Susana Rinaldi

D'aventures en aventures
Elsie Parker and the Poor People of Paris

Summertime
Angelique Kidjo

Paride ed Elena : "Le belle immagini"
Christoph Willibald Gluck, Magdalena Kozená

Pergolesi: Salve regina in F Minor
Giovanni Battista Pergolesi, Véronique Gens

La vie en rose
The Tiger Lilies

She Acts Like a Woman Should
Marilyn Monroe

Hello, Dolly!
Barbra Streisand, Louis Armstrong

Sentimental Journey
Frank Sinatra

Na Rua Do Silêncio – Fado Alexandrino
Mariza

Ce qui me manque
Julio Iglesias

Cold Song
Sting

La dolce vita / La bella melanconica
Nino Rota

Relax ay voo
Line Renaud, Dean Martin

Anne van der Zwaag

She's Always a Woman
Billy Joel

Sweet Mother
Prince Nico Mbarga

I'll Be Your Baby Tonight
Bob Dylan

Good Vibrations
The Beach Boys

Amor Di Mundo
Nancy Vieira

We Don't Run
Willie Nelson

Fix You
Coldplay

Homeward Bound
Simon & Garfunkel

Supergirl
Reamonn

I'm Your Man
Leonard Cohen

Rendez-vous
Alpha Blondy

'Cause I Love You
Johnny Cash

Just Breathe
Pearl Jam

She's a Rainbow
The Rolling Stones

Something
The Beatles

Blue Tangos
Paolo Conte

Home
Edward Sharpe & The Magnetic Zeros

Don't Let Me Be Misunderstood
Nina Simone

Blue Hawaii
Elvis Presley

Green, Green Grass of Home
Coby Grant

Perfect Song
Solomon Burke

The Old-Fashioned Way
Charles Aznavour

One Love
Bob Marley

Paper Aeroplane
Angus & Julia Stone

The Blower's Daughter
Damien Rice

Love Street
The Doors

Beautiful Day
U2

Don't Fence Me In
Bing Crosby

Homeless
Ladysmith Black Mambazo

Home Again
Michael Kiwanuka

Frank Visser

Ain't Got No – I Got Life
Nina Simone

Killing Me Softly with His Song
Fugees

Don't Worry Be Happy
Bobby McFerrin

Bad Things
Jace Everett

It's Too Late
Carole King

Somebody That I Used To Know
Gotye

La La La
Naughty Boy

Paradise by the Dashboard Light
Meat Loaf

't Is stil in Amsterdam
Ramses Shaffy

Space Oddity
David Bowie

Gracias a la vida
Mercedes Sosa

Farewell, Angelina
Joan Baez

Big Yellow Taxi
Joni Mitchell

Diamonds on the Soles of Her Shoes
Paul Simon

Hurry, Mama, Hurry! (Khawuleza)
Miriam Makeba

American Pie
Madonna

Another Brick in the Wall
Pink Floyd

Heading for a Fall
Vaya Con Dios

Lose Yourself to Dance
Daft Punk

Papa Was a Rolling Stone
The Temptations

Son of a Preacher Man
Dusty Springfield

Make Me Smile (Come up and See Me)
Steve Harley

Clandestino
Manu Chao

Back to Black
Amy Winehouse

Look What They've Done to My Song, Ma
Melanie

Wen er maar aan
Anouk

Lovin' You
Minnie Riperton

Mijn vlakke land
Jacques Brel

Once in a Lifetime
Talking Heads

Ana Losa Ramalho

O Romance De Diogo Soares
Fausto

O Barco Vai de Saída
Fausto

A Noite Passada
Sergio Godinho

Sempre Ausente
António Variacões

É P'ra Amanhã
António Variacões

Encosta-te A Mim
Jorge Palma

Afro-Xula
B Fachada

Zorro
António Zambujo

Desfado
Ana Moura

Não Quero Nem Saber
Ana Moura

Saia Rodada
Carminho

Um Contra O Outro
Deolinda

O meu amor
António Zambujo, Carminho

Vodka e Valium 10
Katia Guerreiro

Haja o que houver
Madredeus

Canção verdes anos
Carlos Paredes

Cantigas do maio
Carlos do Carmo & Bernardo Sasseti

Venham mais cinco
Cristina Branco

Agora é que é
Ana Moura

Bairro do oriente
Rui Veloso

Inquietação
JP Simões

Memórias
Rodrigo Leão

Melodia n°2
Carlos Paredes

Os meninos de Huambo
Paulo Carvalho, António Zambujo

125 azul
Trovante

Estou além
Humanos

Lisboa mulata
Dead Combo

Vida nova
Ana Bacalhau

7 colinas
Oquestrada

Carta
Toranja

Babette Kulik

Black Betty
Ram Jam

Feeling Good
Nina Simone

Kung Fu Fighting
Carl Douglas

Walk This Way
Run-D.M.C., Aerosmith

Hit 'Em Up Style (Oops!)
Blue Cantrell

Devil Take My Soul
Sone of Dave

Golden Brown
The Stranglers

Fuck Me Pumps
Amy Winehouse

Young Parisians
Adam & The Ants

Groove Is in the Heart
Deee-Lite

Viva Las Vegas
Elvis Presley

Lo quiere todo
Mano De Dios

Lovefool
The Cardigans

Breathe – Rap Version
Blue Cantrell

Close to Me
The Cure

Walk on the Wild Side
Lou Reed

Oh My God
Mark Ronson, Lily Allen

Spanish Bombs
The Clash

Rapture
Blondie

Whole Lotta Shakin' Going On
Jerry Lee Lewis

Back to Black
Amy Winehouse

Handbags & Gladrags
Rod Stewart

Bar Italia
Pulp

Dance Me to the End of Love
Leonard Cohen

Why Do We Do It?
Mano De Dios

Ziggy Stardust
David Bowie

Je t'aime moi non plus
Serge Gainsbourg, Jane Birkin

What's Happened to Soho?
The Correspondents

Piano Trio No.2 in E Flat Major
Stuttgart Piano Trio

Flore de Brantes

The Girl in the Other Room
Diana Krall

Highway to Hell
Carla Bruni

Dream a Little Dream of Me
Ella Fitzgerald, Louis Armstrong

Pavane pour une infant défunte
Maurice Ravel

Gnossienne: No. 1
Erik Satie

Czech Suite
Antonín Dvořák

Bang Bang (My Baby Shot Me Down)
Nancy Sinatra

La vie en rose
Grace Jones

Como el agua
Paco de Lucía

Entre dos aguas
Paco de Lucía, Manolo Sanlucar

Strong
London Grammar

Old and Wise
The Alan Parsons Project

Stand by Me
Seal

Makeba
Jain

Hot Stuff
Donna Summer

Formidable
Stromae

Ain't No Mountain High Enough
Diana Ross

Killing Me Softly with His Song
Roberta Flack

(Sittin' on) the Dock of the Bay
Otis Redding

Don't Know Why
Norah Jones

The Ballad of Lucy Jordan
Marianne Faithfull

Michael Swier

Bird of Prey
Dita Von Teese

La ritournelle
Sébastien Tellier

I'll Be Seeing You
Françoise Hardy

Glory Box
Portishead

Ibifornia – Noche De Solaris Mix
Cassius

Money Money
Joel Grey, Liza Minnelli

Messiah, "I Know That My Redeemer Liveth"
Kiri Te Kanawa

Heaven
The Rolling Stones

Canopée
Polo & Pan

Prettiest Virgin
Agar Agar

Tiny Tears
Tindersticks

Girls on Film - Night Version
Duran Duran

Fête de trop
Eddy de Pretto

You Oughta Know
Alanis Morissette

Teardrop
Massive Attack

Je suis venu te dire que je m'en vais
Serge Gainsbourg

Hey Joe
Charlotte Gainsbourg

Into My Arms
Nick Cave & The Bad Seeds

Hurt
Johnny Cash

Fast Car
Tracy Chapman

Paradise by the Dashboard Light
Meat Loaf

Eenzame Kerst
André Hazes

Zeg maar niets meer
André Hazes

Vrijgezel
Benny Neyman

Candida Zanelli

Hallelujah
Leonard Cohen

Alexandra Leaving
Leonard Cohen

Here It Is
Leonard Cohen

Boogie Street
Leonard Cohen

The Land of Plenty
Leonard Cohen

Undertow
Leonard Cohen

Morning Glory
Leonard Cohen

On That Day
Leonard Cohen

I Got It Bad and That Ain't Good
Keith Jarrett

Piazza Grande
Lucio Dalla

Summertime
Louis Armstrong

La canzone di Marinella
Fabrizio De André

Bocca di rosa
Fabrizio De André

Amore che vieni amore che vai
Fabrizio De André

La balata di Michè
Fabrizio De André

Il Pescatore
Fabrizio De André

What a Little Moonlight Can Do
Billie Holiday

DIMORESTUDIO

Out of Time
Blur

Le temps de l'amour
Françoise Hardy

State Trooper
Bruce Springsteen

Ain't No Mountain High Enough
Marvin Gaye, Tammi Terrell

New York, I Love You but You're Bringing Me Down
LCD Soundsystem

Sunny
Bobby Hebb

It Can't Be Wrong
Bette Davis

I've Written a Letter to Daddy
Bette Davis

Futura
Lucio Dalla

O Superman
Laurie Anderson

Tasha Marks

Day Too Soon
Sia

In a Manner of Speaking
Nouvelle Vague

Soda Shop
Jay Brannan

The Moss
Cosmo Sheldrake

Postcards from Italy
Beirut

Riptide
Vance Joy

From Nowhere
Dan Croll

Just Like Heaven
The Cure

Lovesong
The Cure

Dancing with Myself
Nouvelle Vague

Golden Years
David Bowie

Don't Wanna Fight
Alabama Shakes

Shape of You
Ed Sheeran

Fastlove, Pt. 1
George Michael

Edge of Seventeen
Stevie Nicks

Love Never Felt So Good
Michael Jackson

Desire
Years & Years

Duck Sauce
Barbra Streisand

It Don't Mean a Thing
Ella Fitzgerald

Magalenha
Sérgio Mendes

Don't Speak
No Doubt

Jive Man
The Correspondents

Lone Digger
Caravan Palace

Fel dev av garden
Movits!

Chambermaid Song
Parov Stelar

Catgroove
Parov Stelar

Lovefool
The Cardigans

Useful Websites and Addresses

Marc Hertrich & Nicolas Adnet
Studio MHNA
5, Passage Piver
Paris
FRANCE
www.studiomhna.com

The Negresco Hotel
37, Promenade des Anglais
06000 Nice
FRANCE
www.hotel-negresco-nice.com

Anne van der Zwaag
www.objectrotterdam.com

Simone Post
www.simonepost.nl

Beatrice Waanders
www.thesoftworld.com

Isaac Monté
www.isaacmonte.nl

Frank Visser
www.ijmcolour.nl

Ana Losa Ramalho
L de Luz
Rua de Miguel Bombarda 469
4050-382 Porto
PORTUGAL
www.ldeluz.com

Jimmy van Gent
White Rabbit Interior
www.instagram.com/whiterabbitinterior

Babette Kulik
Kulik Selzer
www.kulikselzer.com

Flore de Brantes
Galerie Flore
Rue de la Vallée / Dalstraat 40
1050 Brussels
BELGIUM
www.galerieflore.com

Thong Lei
Decoration Empire
Meridiaan 53 – 59
2801 DA Gouda
THE NETHERLANDS
www.decorationempire.nl

Michael Swier
Zomers Bloemen
Van Oldenbarneveltstraat 144
3012 GX Rotterdam
THE NETHERLANDS
www.zomersbloemen.nl

Candida Zanelli
Via Sardegna 36
Milan 20146
ITALY
www.candidazanelli.it

Judith van Mourik
Van Nelleweg 1
3044 BC Rotterdam
THE NETHERLANDS
www.judithvanmourik.nl

Tasha Marks
AVM Curiosities
www.avmcuriosities.com

MANY THANKS TO

Ingrid Robers

Beatrice De Keyzer
Niels Famaey

Jan Kooiman
Anneke Kooiman

Everyone I had the
pleasure to interview.

Bussaco Palace
Hélène Seropian
Laura Durr Alarcon
Gallery 25
Dusty Deco
Jacksons
Morentz
DIMORESTUDIO
Sé
Parc Broekhuizen
Leighton House
Alexandra Schijf

This book is
MARKED

MARKED is an initiative by Lannoo Publishers.
www.marked-books.com

JOIN THE MARKED COMMUNITY on @booksbymarked

Or sign up for our MARKED newsletter with news about new and forthcoming publications on art, interior design, food & travel, photography and fashion as well as exclusive offers and MARKED events on www.marked-books.com.

Author: Patrick Kooiman
Editing: Patrick Lennon
Photography: Patrick Kooiman and Ingrid Robers
Graphic design: Ingrid Robers

If you have any questions or comments about the material in this book, please do not hesitate to contact our editorial team: markedteam@lannoo.com.

© Lannoo Publishing, 2018
D/2018/45/98 – NUR 450/454
ISBN: 978 94 014 4270 1

#AREYOUMARKED

Hello dear reader, I'd love to hear from you! Go to interiorator.com/volume and share photos of how you've applied the lessons from the style experts featured in this book.